THE
BUSINESS
TRANSITION
HANDBOOK

THE BUSINESS TRANSITION HANDBOOK

HOW TO AVOID SUCCESSION PITFALLS
AND CREATE VALUABLE EXIT OPTIONS

LAURIE R. BARKMAN

Published by JWC Publishing
Pittsburgh, Pennsylvania
www.thebusinesstransitionhandbook.com

Printed in the United States of America

Library of Congress Control Number: 2023906539
ISBN Hardcover: 978-1-959508-00-7
ISBN Softcover: 978-1-959508-01-4
ISBN Ebook: 978-1-959508-02-1

This book is dedicated to the three most important people in my life.

Martin, my husband and partner on our life's journey—your love, support, and steadfast encouragement is unbelievable.

Caroline, my talented daughter—you inspire me to make creative connections and a meaningful impact.

Lars, my insightful son—you show me how powerful resilience and intention can be.

TABLE OF CONTENTS

INTRODUCTION

You can't connect the dots looking forward, you can only
connect them looking backwards. So you have to trust
that the dots will somehow connect in your future . . .

STEVE JOBS

Transition.

I've been focused on this theme for a long time. I've devoted
considerable amounts of time to thinking through how enterprises can
navigate the complex process of moving from one chapter to another.
Transition was a critical part of my CEO experience and what led me to
becoming, what a colleague called, "the business transition sherpa."

For most of my career, I've been an operator in a wide range of companies, from small to big. I was hired from the outside to run a subsidiary

of a third-generation privately held company. We sold the business to a global company.

Being part of the deal team process and post-acquisition integration is what first launched me on my journey as a transition and Mergers and Acquisitions (M&A) advisor.

After leaving my executive position, I went into private equity and was on the other side of the deal table.

Now I help business owners plan their successful transitions and benefit by letting the company go on their terms.

Going through the M&A process was exciting, stressful, and an incredibly powerful learning experience. It gave me an appreciation for not only the mechanics, but also the emotional nature of the process. It was a complicated process, and we also had to continue to run the business and keep our foot on the gas pedal at the same time.

Because of my experience working with startups and small companies across my career, I tend to specialize in the lower middle market, though I've also worked with several larger companies. I've been lucky to wear many hats as a business coach, advisor, and adjunct professor of entrepreneurship at Carnegie Mellon University. I've even had the opportunity to add "podcaster" to my resume as the host of *Succession Stories*, where I've spoken with hundreds of experts and entrepreneurs.

This book represents a snapshot of what I've learned over the course of my career and from these conversations focused on how to successfully execute a business transition. I will offer action-oriented ideas throughout this book. As you go through, I will suggest some things for you to think about and to hold yourself accountable to.

The most common way I've heard entrepreneurs and business owners describe themselves is "un-hireable." They might say that an entrepreneur is somebody who will do anything not to get a regular job.

Many entrepreneurs can't bear the thought of working forty hours a week for someone else—but spend *eighty* hours a week working for themselves. Is this you?

And there's no real respite even when your head hits the pillow at night. That's when countless questions begin to run through your mind.

In the beginning, those questions may be, *Am I going to be able to make payroll? Do I know what I'm doing? How long before my savings run out?*

But over time, new considerations and new types of questions creep in.

- *Who will take over for me one day?*
- *What is my business worth?*
- *Should I sell? Who would want to buy it?*
- *Is my business ready? Am I?*
- *What's holding me back?*
- *What would make my business more valuable?*
- *When should I start planning how and when I will leave my business?*
- *What should I be doing now to get ready?*

These questions are complex, dwelling in the gray area where easy answers elude us. That's why I work with owners to help answer these kinds of questions through a focused process of exit value planning. As a business transition sherpa, I guide privately held small to mid-sized businesses from transition to transaction.

My goal is for you to have a more transferable and valuable business. And, for you to think not only about your Now, but also your Next.

The reality is that 80 percent of business owners would like to stop working in their business in the next five to ten years.[1] But this wish is rarely in the form of a concrete plan with milestones, metrics, or a clear timeline. It's just an idea taking shape in our minds, even though it's difficult to wrap our heads around.

Take solace that if this sounds like you, you're not alone. In fact, the Exit Planning Institute has found that less than half of owners had a written and communicated plan.

Not having a plan runs completely counter to the way most owners approach building their business. The data suggests that owners tend to be much better at getting *into* business than getting out. I have some ideas on why that might be.

It can be hard to let your mind leap to what's next when your name is is on the door and your identity is tightly tied into what you have created.

Many founders say that their company is their baby. When you've poured your heart and soul into your baby, it is hard to walk away.

Many owners do not take the time to think truly and meaningfully about what the next step would look like on a day-to-day basis. We might have a faint notion of sitting on corporate boards, investing in new businesses, giving back to the community, or taking a sailboat around the world. But have you considered what it would be like if you were no longer rushing off to the office or checking your overflowing email inbox? How will you fill that time and maintain your sense of identity without a job to rush off to?

There are an infinite number of ways you can share your time, talent, and treasure. Creating a separate identity from your business and having a purpose you are excited about are the "pull factors" that form the pathway to your Next. Maybe you're excited for new adventures, like driving cross-country in a motorhome, or flying to faraway places. Bolstering relationships with family and friends may be your focus. You could serve on non-profit boards for causes you care about, or mentor other business owners as an advisory board member or consultant. With your entrepreneurial experience, you might start another business. Or become an investor in early-stage companies.

I advise owners on how to make these pull factors a reality by building more valuable, saleable businesses. And in my work as a Mergers and Acquisitions advisor, I guide owners through the complex process of letting go . . . a significant ask when you have completely poured your energy, soul, capital, focus, and time into something that feels like a part of you.

You'll come away from reading this book with stories, insights, and examples and a greater understanding of how to:

- Recognize each step of the company lifecycle trajectory
- Identify the difference between readiness and attractiveness as it pertains to your enterprise
- Deliberately think through your future plans for your organization, including how to give yourself more options for a successful transition to new leadership

- Asses the value drivers to inform your value building strategy
- Develop a roadmap through a powerful process of exit value planning

My goal is that this book will reach entrepreneurs, founders, next generation leaders, external hires, and the professionals who help you make decisions about taxes, legal matters, and your financial future. All of us share an interest in your success.

Ultimately, this book will serve as a handbook to business owners and entrepreneurs on how to approach the challenges of leaving their business one day, by letting go of their ventures on their own terms, creating exit options, and transitioning to their next chapter.

This book will provide value to:

- Business owners considering a future exit
- Entrepreneurs looking for value growth strategies
- Leaders thinking about transition options

In this book I will:

1. Outline challenges of business transition in context of value building and exiting on your own terms.
2. Share lessons learned from a wide range of business leaders and experts on the successes and challenges of business transitions and exits.
3. Provide actionable take-aways and tools you can use to create your exit strategy.

Where do we start? How do we map out where we're headed, and how do we get there?

One of the most important things my clients value about working with me is gaining clarity. Holding ourselves to a process. I hold myself and my clients accountable to a plan that we develop. With valuable tools that you may not have access to on your own. That's my role as the business transition sherpa.

I've written this book with the same mindset that I have with all my clients. I don't have all the answers for you, but I will ask challenging questions. My intent is to help you think differently about business transitions, and help you see what you're not seeing yet (but need to).

You built your business, but you haven't done it by yourself. Likewise, when you're starting to think about a transition journey, you're not going to work on this by yourself.

With my coaching clients, I ask "What can I do to be helpful to you right now?" That is the same spirit I have sought to bring to this project.

Or, if you need more time and headspace, that's okay. This is a resource to use on your timeline. Come back to the book from time to time if it moves you to do so. As a companion to the book, I've created a Business Transition Toolkit with all of the exercises in one-place. Download by visiting www.thebusinesstransitionhandbook.com.

I hope that you enjoy this actionable, practical guide with insights gathered from more than 100 entrepreneurs and business experts to help you avoid top succession pitfalls and create more valuable exit options.

Laurie R. Barkman
April 2023

CHAPTER 1

HOW TO GET THE MOST
FROM THIS BOOK

The best time to plant a tree is twenty
years ago. Second-best is today.

CHINESE PROVERB

Here's the good news. The investment you make to get your business ready for an eventual transition is building business value, which is going to pay off for you in the future. You're inherently building the value of your company. All the ideas in this book are meant to be ideas that benefit you TODAY as well as TOMORROW.

A business owner survey[2] asked the question, "What's standing in the way of your exit?" The number one answer was the need to improve the business. Owners didn't feel ready to make an exit until their metrics where were they needed to be.

Ideally, you're starting transition planning when time is on your side. If you have a five-year time horizon, perhaps you have already started. If you have a two-year time horizon, time is short. Let's start developing your plan.

Here are some suggestions to make the most of this book:

1. **Read the chapters in order.** Each chapter addresses a different succession pitfall, and the concepts build on each other throughout the book.

2. **Read all the way through.** Even if you don't think a particular chapter relates to you, there may be a concept or story you will benefit from.

3. **Make it your own.** Complete the exercises in the book. Mark it up. Highlight. Underline. Take notes in the margins. Use sticky notes to easily jump back to important ideas.

4. **Write down key learnings.** You will discover a broad range of topics including strategy, marketing, finance, operations, and

M&A. Examples and anecdotes help bring them to life. Additional concepts and ideas may resonate with you. Write them in the chapter summary sections so that you can recall them later.

5. **Take action.** Each chapter ends with space for action planning. Write down your ideas about how to address the opportunities and challenges spotlighted in the book.

6. **Connect.** Connect with me to receive a digital Business Transition Toolkit with all of the exercises from this book by visiting: www.thebusinesstransitionhandbook.com

CHAPTER 2

YOUR TRANSITION MINDSET AFFECTS YOUR ACTIONS

To begin with the end in mind means to start with a clear understanding of your destination. It means to know where you're going so that you better understand where you are now and so that the steps you take are always in the right direction.

STEPHEN R. COVEY

C onsider this: 100 percent of us are going to leave our company one day. But only a small percentage of business owners have a plan for a transition. Planning for exit is not typically something business owners do when you're in launch, build, or growth mode. You're busy running the business.

Another reason why business owners often neglect to prepare for their exit is the constant grind of running a company, which can be exhausting. Over time, this can lead to a sudden reaction from the owner, which is the biggest threat to business value. How an owner feels about exiting their company creates a "transition mindset."

My observation is that business owners typically fall into one of two categories. The first group wants to run away from the business due to reasons like boredom, burnout, illness, or skill gaps. The second group runs toward the next chapter of their life, whether it be retirement or starting a new venture. Your transition mindset and what drives your motivation to exit will be influenced by your specific circumstances.

Unfortunately, more negative exit motivations, or "push factors," can lead to a reduction in the value of the business, leaving you without the time and inclination to plan your exit and enhance your outcome.

So why am I advocating for you to be thinking about your future transition or liquidity event to sell your business?

Because for many owners, it is like swimming in a murky pond. You can't see where you're headed with your business, and it feels uncomfortable not finding a way to leave the water. This is a common discussion I have with guests on my *Succession Stories Podcast*. Entrepreneurs share their succession stories—some expressed regrets in their transition experience, while others celebrated success overcoming obstacles along the way. What I noticed from these conversations is that planning goes a long way toward making your vision come to life. There are many paths that you can take. Choosing which one is best for you is a great place to start.

Potential exit strategies:

- step back from the day-to-day
- take some chips off the table by bringing in an investor
- sell the business to a third-party
- pass the business to the next generation of family
- sell the business to management
- retire from business
- stay on as a consultant, advisor, or board member

What is the reason to develop an exit strategy even if your timeline is ten-plus years away? Here's the amazing secret: all the things you need to prepare for an exit will enable you to run a more profitable and enjoyable business! So why wouldn't you want to do that?

What you'll learn in this book is that regardless of your exit plan, you will be creating value in your business by avoiding common transition pitfalls. By following the guidance in these chapters, you can impact the value of your business while time is still on your side to make necessary changes.

Some entrepreneurs have a mountain climber mentality. They built a business, moved on, and want to do it all over again. Seeking the challenge and thrill of the next mountain top journey.

It can be challenging to determine when the right time is to let go . . . especially when your growth is accelerating.

Bill Prinzivalli learned this all too well, experiencing a rollercoaster of the highest and lowest points in his company. Bill started Prince Software in 1986 and eventually specialized in solving Y2K systems issues for Fortune 1000 companies. At its peak in 1998, they grew to fifty people, with nineteen international distributors, $10 million in revenue, and a $30 million valuation. With the exciting rise of the Y2K industry, Bill rode the wave but waited too long to execute an exit strategy. As the company's growth potential diminished, so did its value. I've coined a term called the "not now mentality" because I encounter it often.

A married couple in their sixties owns a professional services firm. One of them faced health issues several years ago which made them start thinking about a business transition. For years, they had talked about selling but they always concluded, "not now." We met to discuss their goals and where they are on the readiness continuum. They shared, "We're really starting to think about it. But our challenge is when we do sell, we won't have that annuity stream anymore and we're not sure what that looks like for us." Their self-imposed obstacles are likely to continue without their focus on transferability and salability of the business. By the time they finally become "ready to sell," they may not be "sell-ready."

One of my podcast listeners is the founder of a marketing agency. She reached out to share her intention to replace herself as CEO. She successfully hired an outside CEO and transitioned day-to-day responsibilities enabling her to focus on the bigger picture for the company. From a life stage standpoint, she wants to develop a portfolio of businesses and enjoy time with her child. What's her strategic transition timeline? Around ten years. Currently she's in her thirties. Maybe one day she will share her succession story on my podcast.

When should you start thinking about business transition planning and working on things in earnest? Depending on your specific circumstances, it could be seven to ten years ahead of an intended transition.

Not all companies will successfully pass on to a new owner. Here are some statistics that might surprise you.

According to the U.S. Bureau of Labor Statistics, approximately 20 percent of new businesses fail during the first two years of founding, 45 percent within the first five years, and 65 percent within the first 10 years. Only 25 percent of businesses make it to 15 years or more. These statistics haven't changed much over time and have been consistent since the 1990s.[3] Additionally, survey data shows that only 20 percent of small businesses listed for sale actually sell.[4]

There are several reasons why businesses don't sell, or make it past their 10th birthday:

1. **The company is not worth what the owner needs to exit.** It's possible the owner may have unrealistic expectations due to anecdotal valuation assumptions about similar companies in their industry. More commonly it is because the business is not worth what the owner needs to sustain their lifestyle outside of the business.

2. **There are inherent flaws that exist.** If the company is losing money, is outgunned in the market, or has cash flow issues, a buyer won't be excited about its prospects.

3. **Lack of transferability.** A common challenge is transferability. Without the owner, some companies are not able to survive a change of hands. An owner who is deeply involved in the business day-to-day, serving in operations, customer service, and/or sales role, needs to ensure that the business can thrive without them at the helm. A business that isn't transferable has more risk, and likely to yield a lower price than desired.

If you don't have a transition plan, what's the likelihood you will get the outcome you want?

Dr. Gail Matthews, a psychology professor at Dominican University in California found that you are 42 percent more likely to achieve your goals just by writing them down. Other neuroscience studies have shown that people who vividly describe their goals in writing experience greater goal success.

Before we develop your goals, the first activity I suggest will baseline your "transition mindset."

I use this exercise in workshops that I lead with CEOs and business owners across the country. At the start of each session, I introduce the word "transition" and ask for the first words that come to mind. The brainstorming helps break the ice and informs me about the mindset of the room. After writing up the words on the flipchart, we discuss whether the words have a positive, negative, or neutral connotation to the group.

Transition Mindset Exercise:

1. What comes to mind when you think about transition? Review the following list of words and circle the ones most relevant to you.

Adoption	Emotional	Integrate	Necessary
Acquisition	Enlightening	Interruption	Needed
Adaptive	Evaluate	Invigorating	Negative
Anxiety	Event	Knowledge	New
Challenging	Evolve	transfer	New
Change	Evolving /	Learning curve	perspective
Complete	evolution	Leaving	Next chapter
overhaul	Exciting	Letting go	Next generation
Constant	Exit	Liberating	Not easy
Continuity	Fading	Lifestyle	Now
Control	Fear	Management	Opportunity
Creating new	Finance	Merging	Organize
profit centers,	Fun	Metamorphosis	Pain
services	Future	Millennials	Pass along
Culture	Generations	Misery	Passing on
Cyclical	Growth	Mistakes	People
Deliberate	Happiness	Modernizing	Personnel
Destination	Hard	Money	Phases
Development	Hope	Move	Pivoting
Different	Humility	Moving on	Preparation
Different	Improve	Movement	Processes
Difficult	Improvement	Moving into	Reaction
Disruptive	Inevitability	new role	Resistance
Diversification	Infrastructure	Multi-genera-	Retirement
Easy	Intentional	tional	

Risk of standing still	Shift / shifting	Sustainability	Uncertainty
	Slow	Terrible	Unexpected
Responsibilities	Smooth	Time	Upward
Roles	Soul searching	Tomorrow	Visionary
Scary	Stability	Training	Wealth
Selling the business	Structured	Transfer	Work
	Succession	Transformation	

2. Group like words together to create categories. Pick three to five words and write them in the table below. Consider how these words make you feel. Do they have a positive, neutral, or negative connotation? Write down why you feel that way.

Transition Word	Negative	Neutral	Positive
1.			
2.			
3.			
4.			
5.			

Positive words are an indication that you're open minded. You're thinking about transition and change in a positive way.

Negative words could indicate that you're not looking forward to this process. Power through, my friend. It will get better!

One entrepreneur described transition as a switch over. She said, "I think it gives the feeling there is some sort of movement. It's not always natural, but sometimes it can be a natural progression." Now that's a transition mindset.

What does transition mean to you? It means a lot of things to us at different times. Transition is movement. Transition alludes to a process that this is part of something.

The reason I call myself the business transition sherpa is because I see entrepreneurship as a journey and there's a natural progression. I use the analogy of a sherpa because I don't have all the answers, I have a process. In this book, I'll be with you on this journey and support you.

A big question that you'll need to address one day is how do founders, business owners, entrepreneurs, and next generation family leaders, define the end goal? Fundamentally, transition is about change above all—whether a change of control or a change of ownership. It's a change of how you're running or consuming yourself with your business.

A survey from the Business Enterprise Institute (BEI) found that only 20 percent of business owners have a written exit plan.[5] Even if a plan is written down, many times it's not widely communicated. If it's just in your head and not clearly laid out in a written blueprint that others can see, is it really a plan?

I think of business transition as having three **Strategic Readiness Pillars**—business, personal, and financial. All three pillars need to be in balance. And it can be hard to keep all three in balance.

Here is an overview—we'll dive into more detail on these concepts in later chapters.

Business Readiness Strategies are about managing risk, transferability, and growth and positioning the company for a potential transition as well as having a written and communicated plan.

Financial Readiness Strategies are about knowing your requirements for what you need to satisfy the lifestyle you want to have after you exit your business. It also includes understanding what the business is worth and the total picture of your net worth. For many business owners, the company is 80 percent to 90 percent of their net worth.

Personal Readiness Strategies focus on your transition. Your ability to separate yourself from the business. Your ability to create pull factors, aspects of your life that pull you forward and make you excited about your next thing.

We don't always want to think about the end. Quoting Stephen Covey, what if we "begin with the end in mind." Sometimes it can play to your strengths to do that. We can see a connection between having a transition mindset and business value.

So how does this tie to business value?

Just like people, companies have a life cycle from birth to death. The best time to sell your business is when your business is in the healthy adult stage.

If you have a health concern, get divorced, are dealing with the death of a co-owner, or have a partner dispute, you might be thinking about a change of ownership. A personal crisis could lead to the decision to close the business or liquidate tangible assets for market value. If you're approaching a sale of the business as it is turning downward, the business will not be worth much. The best time to exit is when your business is doing well, not in decline—or worse, freefall.

Based on an analysis of 1,511 business owners and their companies, The Value Builder System found that the owner's personal reason for exit, and the actions they have personally taken to exit, play a significant role in the value of their business.

When comparing two similar businesses in the same geography and industry and of a similar size, if each owner has different reasons for exiting, they will likely have drastically different business values. Other factors that can impact the value of the business include the owner's steps to prepare for exit and the proportion of shares owned. When added up, these factors can predict up to 53% of the difference in the value of two seemingly similar businesses.[6]

There are lots of reasons why people would be afraid of exit planning. Change can feel uncomfortable. We like to deal with what we know. We like certainty.

If you're the rainmaker in your company, and you've got people counting on you for paychecks, it's hard to think about anything else but running your business. It may not necessarily be a negative feeling about exit planning, it just might be that you are really, truly not ready to change.

It's hard to get business owners to think about transition planning until they're ready. It might take a spouse, business partner, or an advisor like me to have that conversation with you.

If there are multiple owners accountable to one another, it is important to develop a transition plan well in advance of a succession crisis.

An $8 million revenue professional services firm reached out to discuss the sale of the business. When I asked what drove their interest, they shared that half of their partners left the firm over the past year due to resignations, retirements, and an unexpected death. These exits not only impacted the business financially due to partner buyout provisions, they also hampered internal succession and ownership plans for the future. In sharing this example, my message is that it is important to work proactively, or you could face downward pressure on your sale price.

There may be more negative reasons why maybe we want to transition our business. Examples of "push factors" for an exit include:

- Family fights
- Death of business partner or family member
- Death of sole owner
- Business downturn
- Divorce
- Partnerships dissolving
- Owner burnout
- Health issues
- Market factors

Think about all the recessions that we've been through. Some business owners survived the challenges of 2008 only to be hit with the whammy of COVID-19 in 2020. The lesson is that we never know what "Black Swan" event can come along to disrupt our carefully laid plans—which is why giving yourself more options and more possibilities is the best safeguard against disruption. The more options you can create, the more likely you reach the outcome you desire.

In my client advisory sessions, I like to ask my clients what they reflected on and what they liked best about our time together. One of my clients said, "You've been really getting me to think differently about my pull factors and my push factors."

I had worked with another client, Don (not his real name), on a personal readiness questionnaire. In this assessment, there are four dimensions that we measure with a point value of 0 to 100. On the first dimension, "Vision for the Future," Don scored a zero. He was not able to answer the questions: *What will I do next? What will I do after I leave my business?*

This is often a challenge for founders or family members if your name is on the door. Your identity is so tied in also because of your community standing, your pride, and relationships with your employees. All those things keep your identity strong, but they can also hold you back from envisioning a different reality for yourself.

When it comes to developing your personal identity away from your business, it is good to take note of how you spend your time and who you spend it with. Do most of your social interactions outside of work involve your work colleagues?

Is there something you aspire to do more of outside of work? If you sold your business, and had the funds to support your lifestyle what would you choose to do?

Here are some "pull factors" entrepreneurs shared with me on *Succession Stories*. After leaving their business, they chose to:

- Buy another company to operate
- Become a minority investor with acquisition entrepreneurs
- Launch a startup
- Create a family office for investing
- Create a family foundation for philanthropy
- Launch a venture fund
- Focus on real estate investing
- Be a grandparent

- Work with other business owners as a consultant or advisor
- Serve on boards
- Live abroad

These are all positive examples. The more things you look forward to, the more you will work to achieve your transition goals.

"Launching a Family Office"
Alex Panosian, CW Growth Partners
Succession Stories Podcast E73[7]

Alex Panosian and his father started CW Growth Partners as a family invest-ment office focused on acquiring, leading, and growing small businesses in the Midwest. Alex shares his views on the importance of family communications and alignment.

Laurie Barkman:
If someone is contemplating a transition, what they want to do next, what are three things you would say are critical to consider in launching a family office?

Alex Panosian:
First thing, without a doubt is you've got to have alignment in the family. My sister is a very smart woman, has a great professional job. She has a voice, but she's not involved on a day-to-day basis. We had a sit-down conversation with all of us. It was a few hours with my dad, my mom, my wife, and my sister, deciding, "Is this the direction we all really want to go and what does that look like? How does it make sense for us?"

One of the things that's incredibly important is we still want to get along at Thanksgiving. That's like the number one thing that you don't want to screw up. I think to make sure you never reach that point; you must be really intentional with the communications and sometimes cover things that can be a little bit awkward. How do people get paid? Where do the profits go? All of those things are important to cover up front.

Then the second thing I'll say is, that's the higher-level direction, do we want to do this? Are these the roles people are going to play? In our case, I'm coming in as the next generation and playing that role. Or are you going to hire someone outside? What does that look like? What could that look like? Do you want to team up with other family offices? There are a few different networks out there. There are a few different firms that bundle multiple family offices together.

Then the third is what direction do you want to go? How do you want to leverage the expertise of all parties involved? What I mean by that is we talked to some family offices that focus a lot on public equities in the stock market. Some that focus a lot on the industry that they're coming from, and others like us that are trying to grow and diversify, but also stay close enough to what you're doing. In my case, I'm comfortable with small unit leadership, leading teams of ten to fifteen people. Or in my dad's case, running a small business and what that looks like.

─────────── **TAKE-AWAYS:** ───────────

- Having a written plan is essential for achieving the desired outcome in a business transition.
- When considering a business transition, it is important to have a positive mindset, as this can lead to better outcomes.
- Business transition involves three key areas: business readiness, financial readiness, and personal readiness. Consider all three when planning a successful transition.

─────────── **MY ACTION PLAN** ───────────

What are three things that you will do within the next three to six months to become more prepared for business transition? Finishing this book can be one of them!

Action Item	Resources Needed	Start By Date	Complete By Date

CHAPTER 3

YOUR ORGANIZATION NEEDS YOU TOO MUCH

Entrepreneurial management in a new venture requires building a top management team long before the new venture actually needs one and long before it can actually afford one.

PETER DRUCKER

E very entrepreneur brings certain skills to their business to create value. Maybe your passion is product development. Or you love working directly with customers to deliver your service.

Len Caric is a successful acquisition entrepreneur and teaches entrepreneurship at Carnegie Mellon University. "I've been fortunate all my career to primarily deal with small businesses. These businesses are personalities. These are not giant corporations that are faceless. These businesses are who these people are, and the people are who the business is. I have no idea how many hours I work. It just becomes who you are and what you do. You're always thinking about it, but you're also able to balance. It's hard to describe. These businesses have personality because of the people that started them or are running them."[8]

Maybe you're the front facing person in the business and lead the sales effort. You've created long-lasting relationships with your clients that have driven repeat business.

If all decisions in your business—small to big—rest on your shoulders, your business may be stressful to run. You can never take a break.

Some entrepreneurs pride themselves on wearing multiple hats, especially related to their core competency. Even entrepreneurs who grow their businesses to large scales may pride themselves on staying connected to their original talents. Mark Zuckerberg, for example, made a New Year's resolution in 2012 to code each day, to ensure his technology skills stayed relevant even as he oversaw rapid growth of the company.

You may relate to this temptation to keep skin in the game when it comes to your business' core offering. But could this also be holding your business back?

The number one pitfall to be aware of is whether your organization needs you too much. If your organization cannot thrive without you as the owner, the person running the company, your business may not be sellable. For many business owners, this is really bad news.

I conducted a business assessment with the co-founder and CEO of a graphic design and photography company to help her measure risks and strengths in her business. She was surprised by the results. Afterward she said, "You helped me see that I'm holding my company back. I used to think me being one of the main reasons customers work with us was invaluable. Now I understand the fatal flaw in my thinking." That was a pivotal moment.

You might be surprised to know that a business that cannot thrive without its owner is not worth much to a buyer. Why is this?

In exit planning, and getting your company ready for succession or sale, transferability is an important concept. If only one person in your business leads mission critical functions, it could pose risk to your business today, and to a new owner in the future.

For example, some business owners are "rainmakers" for their companies to drive growth. They are responsible for service delivery, product development, sales, or client service. Owners who are rainmakers tend to have strong connections because they are involved in every facet of the customer relationship.

While these relationships can fuel growth initially, over time it will present risk to your business value. Relationship based deals may be verbal agreements rather than papered. Revenue growth will flatline because there are only so many hours in a day, and there may be limits to one person's personal capacity to sell.

Another risk from a rainmaker approach is taking long-standing relationships for granted. An example illustrating this risk is with one of my business services clients. Their company had a few MSAs (Master Service Agreements) in place with large institutional clients for one-time projects. For years, they had an exclusive agreement with one particular client; they were the only firm providing their specific services to the institution. While the MSA did not guarantee work, it led to steady business representing more than 10 percent of annual revenue. In the annual renewal discussion, my client met with the new director of the procurement group. Unfortunately, the institution had signed on three new providers under a non-exclusive MSA and were fully booked for the next 12-months. In that instant, my client's revenue projections went down ten percent. It was a tough lesson to learn that even long-standing relationships can change when you least expect it.

Data from The Value Builder System shows that companies with equity holders who are personally responsible for less than 25 percent of the company's revenue are nearly twice as likely to receive a premium offer of six times earnings before interest, tax, depreciation, and amortization (EBITDA) or higher. In other words, if you are the primary driver of sales in your business, you may be half as likely to receive an offer, and you're more likely to see a discount on the company's value (less than three times EBITDA).[9]

What happens to the business if you leave? Or pass away? Or go on an extended vacation? Will the business suffer to some extent or continue onward without disruption?

"Creating a Business That Can Thrive Without You"
Meredith Meyer Grelli, Co-Founder,
Wigle Wiskey and Threadbare Cider + Mead
Succession Stories E97[10]

Meredith Meyer Grelli is the co-founder of the Wigle Whiskey Distillery. In 2010, Meredith and her family opened a distillery in the city of Pittsburgh, the first since prohibition. Naming their whiskey after the leader of the 1794 Whiskey Rebellion, Phillip Wigle, they needed Pennsylvania's laws to change before opening their doors. Over the past twelve years, their patience and innovation paid off. Wigle has been the most awarded craft whiskey distillery for five consecutive years. Meredith joined me for a conversation on innovation and setting up the organization for sustainable success. Just after this episode was released, it was announced that Meredith's company was being sold to a strategic buyer.

Laurie Barkman:
When did you start to think about stepping away from the day-to-day and how did you make that happen?

Meredith Meyer Grelli:
This happened in stair steps, it wasn't a revelation all at once. For a long time, we felt like we shouldn't be doing the things that we're doing. The level of detail at which we're operating is not good for the business. But we couldn't figure out how to extricate ourselves from some of them. The first step was pre-pandemic, we started developing growth plans for leaders and saying, here's where we want you to be over the next two years. We created those in part by parceling off things that we felt we shouldn't be active in. We said we're going to be patient about this. We're looking at it from a two to three-year view. And then the pandemic happened. All of that accelerated because we're a hospitality business. We're also a manufacturer. When our hospitality operations shut down over the pandemic, we didn't let any full-time team members go. We became much more active in leadership development, feedback, and actively managing people's growth plans.

For me personally, Carnegie Mellon University approached me about a full-time role. I had an adjunct role teaching entrepreneurship courses for a couple of years. Well, now we've got four months to make sure everybody's okay and then I'm going to do it, and that will be the test. We doubled down on the growth plans from spring through summer, and attached financial incentives to the growth to each individual leader. Lo and behold, they all met the growth targets. In the fall, I truly stepped away, because of this new obligation. The business is running better now than when I was trying to micromanage everything, which is a terrible tactic, and one that I employed far too much. Everyone, including all of our team members, and my family, are much happier this way.

In general, there's a lot of risk for businesses that are so tied in with their owner that they can't thrive without them. A key question that we ask clients is "When was the last time you took a vacation?" The follow-up question is, "Did you check email? Did you check in on your phone? Did you really have quality time away?"

What if you weren't in your business for three months? You can be intentional and purposeful to work on this over time. Take a day off and truly unplug.

Then in six months, take two days off. You'll know where the gaps are. Maybe you need to delegate some duties to others. Maybe you need to transition responsibilities and document processes. Eventually you may be able to step away from the business to make sure that the business will be okay and thrive without you.

A different type of owner is "The Architect." The Architect develops a framework that others execute. This will increase the organization's capabilities over time.

It's possible to make a switch from a "rainmaker" to an "architect" owner if you can:

- **Delegate:** Delegate responsibilities that are outside of your skill-set or sap the lifeblood from you.
- **Train:** Hire and train salespeople to do the selling. Training others will expand growth opportunities and enable you to focus on other aspects of the business.
- **Build:** Create processes and systems so that others can do the selling and marketing.

For the past few years, I've led a Strategic Growth Workshop for business owners and CEOs. During the sessions, we've discussed how a business can be less dependent on its owners and I've noted some of the most common responses. They fall into three categories: planning, people, and process. While each idea has their own merit, whether it is a fit for your business depends on your specific situation.

Planning

- Establish a strategic plan
- Develop mission, vision, values
- Succession planning

People

- Expand senior leadership team
- Hire "2IC" second-in-command (General Manager, Sales Leader, Project Manager)
- Cross-training and increase skillset of management team
- Delegation to direct reports
- Create cross-functional leadership team
- Development and training, accelerate learning curve
- Formalized accountability chart, empowering direct reports
- Hiring and structuring roles
- Working with HR and CFO (full-time or outsourced/partial resource)
- Conflict resolution—let managers resolve issues without your steering
- 2IC shadow you on M&A business acquisitions

Process

- Develop more standard practices
- Implement customer focused processes
- Reporting software—operational and financial

Delegation is a critical skill for any business owner. If you are personally overseeing the details, chances are you are a bottleneck to your company's growth and its value. If your goal is to build a business that can thrive without you, you'll want to master the art of delegation.

Start by assigning a degree of autonomy you want your employee to have, and then outline a time-based or financial budget to work within. Finally encourage employees who get stuck to come to you with questions you can simply answer yes or no to, and you'll find the number of problems that end up in your lap will diminish. All the while, you'll be building a more enjoyable and valuable business.

Author Nick Leighton puts it this way, "Time is a commodity for most entrepreneurs, and the best way to treat it as such is by letting go and outsourcing the work that you don't love doing—or work that's beneath your pay grade. At the end of the day, delegating tasks that you don't enjoy doing can impact your business's success.

Business owners tend to do everything, which isn't practical as you grow," says Leighton. "As the business becomes dependent on you, you focus on your passion less and less. You're bogged down with processes and this leads to burnout and prevents your business from growing. Instead, do what you love, outsource the rest."[11]

Now it's your turn. What are ways you can decrease your organization's dependency on you for driving sales, or for overall decision-making?

1. _____

2. _____

3. _____

4. _____

5. _____

This is where distinguishing between how profitable your business and how valuable your business is can come in handy. Some people use profitable and valuable interchangeably but of course they are often in conflict with one another.

Instead of hiring salespeople, the owner seeking to maximize profits would do all the selling themselves. Instead of hiring a management team, they would hire the lowest paid staff they can find to simply execute. While the profit-seeker may maximize their profits, they would also grow a business that may not be sellable.

After growing his medical equipment company to $15 million in revenue, Kevin Trout sold the business to a strategic buyer. One of the critical decisions Kevin made was to build a management team around him. Although it decreased short-term profits, the business was more transferable and increased his enterprise value.

"Preparing Your Business For Sale"
Kevin Trout, Vistage CEO Peer Advisory Board Chair
Succession Stories Podcast E66[12]

Kevin Trout started Grandview Medical Resources with the intent to sell one day. The medical equipment company grew at an impressive rate of 30 percent year over year. But this pace created financial risk in the business and was impacting Kevin's health. Eventually the company grew to $15 million in revenue and sold to a strategic buyer. He shared a perspective on four phases of growth and the trade-offs of decreased short-term profits to increase enterprise value in the longer term.

Laurie Barkman:
If a business owner is thinking about selling their company, what would be three things that you might give them some insights on?

Kevin Trout:
It's never too early to start building value in your business. When I talk about building value it doesn't just mean growing revenues. It doesn't just mean adding staff and people to your org chart. I think you really need to focus on

those eight business drivers that you allude to in your Value Builder Assessment. I wish I would have had the assessment back when I was getting ready to sell because not having that, I didn't have an awareness of some of the areas in which I could have strengthened the company and maybe gotten a little bit more value out of it. I missed that and would encourage everybody to really understand what that entails and start doing it now, even if they're not thinking about selling their business anytime in the near future. Why not build value in your company right now anyway, it doesn't make any sense not to.

I would also understand the business life cycle. Starting a business from scratch and growing it is like driving a manual transmission car. When you're in first gear, you're the owner, you start the company. Your main focus is to go out and get customers and bring in revenue and everybody wears a lot of hats, even though there's only a few people. You get to a certain point where you've got to push in the clutch and shift into second gear. Now you've got some revenue coming in, you've got customers, you start to add some salespeople, you start to add an office admin, you start to get a bookkeeper, whether it's full-time or fractional.

The company starts to grow in second gear. Profits start to appear and they're kind of nice in second gear. If you wait too long, to shift the clutch into third gear, the next thing you know, you have twenty people in there all reporting to the owner. That's not sustainable long-term. Leaders can only really manage maybe six direct reports. When you have ten to twenty now the CEO becomes the bottleneck. The owner becomes the bottleneck to that company's growth.

That's when you push the clutch and shift into third gear. Third gear is when you start to bring in some professional managers. You put a leadership team in place, and he starts to manage the different departments. So you only have your leadership team reporting to the owner or the CEO. The leadership team allows you to grow even more, and that business owner takes one more step away from the day-to-day activity. He's no longer making sales calls, but he will go out and he'll participate in the important sales calls with the salesperson, but he doesn't have any of his own customers anymore.

A lot of owners don't understand what it takes to get into third gear. Because when they start bringing in professional managers, profits start to disappear, and they're definitely afraid of giving up profits. But it's necessary, because when you get to fourth gear, which I call overdrive, profits come back exponentially greater than they were in second gear, and the owner doesn't work in the business anymore. They have a leadership team that does all the tactical work, and the owner is just a strategic visionary, and makes sure that the company is moving in the right direction. But the leadership team is responsible for all the activities and all the tactical day-to-day stuff, and you hold them accountable for the profitability.

Getting to fourth gear is where a lot of business owners hesitate. I gave up my profits when I shifted into third gear, brought in some professional managers. I had a VP of operations, VP of finance, and VP of administration. I still ran the salespeople, but I wasn't selling to anybody directly. I was more involved in the big deals. I couldn't afford those people at the time, but boy did it pay off. We got to fourth gear and my life was so much easier because in fourth gear, you don't have to work forty hours a week. You can put in thirty and have a wonderful work life balance. That's nirvana. Profits are nice, that's the time to sell which is what I did.

The real trick is understanding what the four phases are, and more importantly, knowing when to push in the clutch. The timing is very important because if you push the clutch too soon, you stall the engine. You're spending too much money. If you hesitate to push in the clutch, you wait too long. The tachometer goes in a red zone and people get burned out and the number one person that gets burned out is you—the business owner. I was right there in first and second gear, I should have pushed the clutch in a little sooner. The point is I got into each of the different phases. It all worked out for me, and when I got to fourth gear profits were nice. That was my best income, and I wasn't having to work forty hours a week.

─────────────── **TAKE-AWAYS:** ───────────────

- Transferability, or the ability for a business to continue operating without the presence of its owner, is important in planning for succession or sale.
- A business that relies too heavily on the skills or relationships of its owner may pose a transition risk to the business and its value.
- Steps that business owners can take to decrease organizational dependency on themselves include expanding leadership teams, cross-training and increasing the skillset of management teams, delegation, and standardizing practices.

─────────────── **MY ACTION PLAN** ───────────────

What are three things that you will do within the next three-six months to make your business less dependent upon you?

Action Item	Resources Needed	Start By Date	Complete By Date

CHAPTER 4

WHAT WILL YOU DO AFTER YOU LEAVE THE BUSINESS

All things are difficult before they are easy.

THOMAS FULLER

What will you do after you leave your business? This is a common question business owners have when thinking about their future.

In my conversations with hundreds of business owners, I can tell it is the most overlooked aspect of planning. It's too easy to put off thinking about what your goals are, and how you might achieve them. Maybe it makes you feel selfish or uncomfortable.

According to the Exit Planning Institute (EPI), less than 10 percent of business owners have a formal, written "life after business" plan. Half of owners have no plans in place to cover illness, death, or forced exit.[13]

Even the most affluent and successful founders struggle with one common problem: the regret of how they handled leaving their company. EPI found that many business owners struggle with the exit of their business for a variety of reasons, and that 75 percent of those who exit "profoundly regret" the decision within twelve months of exiting.

As an entrepreneur, you've spent endless hours identifying opportunities to solve problems. You've dedicated your life to building and running a profitable enterprise with an eye toward future exit. And eventually when you leave the business, you may have expectations of a life of leisure and luxury—only to find you regret the decision.

Most owners feel that they get pushed out of their business when they leave. The happiest exits occur when an owner feels that they are pulled to their "next." Pull factors give you reasons to be excited about your next chapter. Pull factors are things you want to do in the future.

Push factors are actual (or perceived) mechanisms that make you feel as if you are being "pushed" out of your business. If you sell the company, the new owner or majority investor may not want you to stay on as

CEO. You might leave the company entirely or become the Chair of the Board—a role that is less operational day-to-day, and more strategic.

How would you handle this change? Would you feel that you were being pushed out, or be excited to move on?

What would you do if you sold your company or spent less time running it day-to-day?

Age Stages Versus Life Stages

Many business owners and entrepreneurs face the challenge of wondering what they will do after they leave the business. In the US, it is common for owners to consider selling when they are between sixty-two and sixty-seven based on eligibility for retirement benefits.

Turning off what is likely a big part of your identity is not an easy task. Often our personal identity is intertwined with our business identity. When you leave, and eventually you will, you may face this critical challenge.

Jerry Cahn believes in leading a fulfilling life throughout different life stages. As chair of Vistage CEO Peer Advisory Boards in New York, Jerry works with owners to find more success in their business and personal lives. He founded AgeBrilliantly.org to help people focus on opportunities for a fulfilling life while working in their company and afterward. Jerry and I talked about how to create a positive mindset by thinking about life stages, rather than age stages.

I've spoken with various entrepreneurs on *Succession Stories* about this sensitive issue, and the emotional aspects can feel devastating if you're not ready for the transition.

"Finding Purpose After Selling The Business"
Sarah Dusek, Co-Founder, Under Canvas and
General Partner, Enygma Ventures
Succession Stories Podcast E94[14]

Founded in 2009, Under Canvas re-defined experiential hospitality in the US growing from their first location in Yellowstone, Montana, to several luxury glamping accommodations near America's most popular national parks. Sarah shared her incredible journey scaling and growing a business from nothing, finding growth capital, to selling it for over $100 million to a private equity firm. Sarah stayed on for a year to transition and reduce the majority control of her company.

"I had a very strong vision and desire to continue growing the company, and a very clear idea about how I was going to do that. But we did not have the same vision around how that was going to unfold. It was heartbreaking honestly, just devastating, that I was not going to continue to stay and lead this company. I led through a transition, but it was probably the worst moment of my life. It's like giving birth to a child. We had been with and grown this company from nothing, zero to hero. I wasn't ready for that journey to end. It was a very painful era. People often say, "Oh, I bet you made a lot of money." Then I say, "Well, you don't know how much money I took out of the company, because you don't know how much of the company was left and was mine, so you don't know what that looks like." I wasn't necessarily ready at that particular moment, so it was a shock and a grief with transitioning away from the day-to-day of a company that I loved, was super passionate about, and still felt like there was a very big journey to still go on."

Your ability to manage this freedom, from a time and emotional standpoint, is critical. When you leave your business, there can be a feeling of loss of identity and community that your business provided to you. Devising a plan before the sale can help improve the chances of a successful transition. Many business owners lack the time to engage in outside hobbies and interests.

According to the National Federation of Independent Business, the largest small business association in the US, 71 percent of members take fewer than ten days of vacation per year, despite the ability to set their own schedules.[15]

A thoughtful transition is a multi-year process that provides you with opportunity to build up non-business-related freedom, purpose, and relationships.

These may include:

- Taking time to rest and contemplate
- Reinvigorating relationships with friends and family
- Identifying values that are of utmost personal importance and matching with appropriate activities
- Revisiting old hobbies or learning new skills
- Engaging in charitable endeavors
- Exercising regularly
- Traveling to places you've always wanted to visit

In the period leading up to a sale or transition, it is recommended that business owners dedicate one day each week to experimenting with new hobbies, spending time with family, or connecting with old friends.

When I first met my client Don, I asked a series of questions about how he envisioned his future once he was no longer in the business. Don was the founder and owner of a commercial plumbing company. His son worked in the business but had not committed to taking over the company from his father. Don was most concerned about the profitability and viability of the business long-term. He was experiencing too much stress and felt that it was time to retire. The market had peaked for his business, and he wanted to diversify his wealth to minimize risk. He was increasingly thinking about cashing out.

We used the Value Builder System PREScore™ (or Personal Readiness to Exit Score) Assessment to baseline his score across key primary drivers. The PREScore is an eight-minute, online questionnaire that evaluates a business owner's readiness to exit their company on a personal level.

The two most important drivers include future vision and personal detachment.

1. **Future Vision**—What do you plan to do after you leave your business?

Why do you want to exit your business? Many owners decide to sell because they need to retire or take care of their health. Those are valid reasons to exit, but they do not necessarily lead to a satisfying result.

The key to maximizing this driver is to become clear on what you are excited to pursue after you leave your business. You should consider what you are most looking forward to in life after your business.

Guests who have come on *Succession Stories* have shared future goals including:

- Step back from the day-to-day
- Take some chips off the table by bringing in an investor (recapitalize)
- Launch or acquire a new company
- Mentor next generation of family
- Retire from business
- Stay on as a consultant or advisor
- Serve as board member

2. **Personal Detachment**—Have you built a fulfilling life outside of your company?

How personally attached to your business are you? Have you built a fulfilling life outside your company? How much of your self-worth is tied up in your role as the owner? It's natural to feel proud of the business you've built. However, being too personally invested in your company can lead to a difficult time transitioning out of it. The secret is to start building up a rewarding life with friends and fulfilling projects outside of your business.

Don's initial score on the questions related to these drivers were zero out of 100 points. He didn't feel great learning what the assessment uncovered. Don's attitude was positive though, and he was motivated to make changes through subsequent transition planning advisory and coaching with me. I encourage you to take the next step and work on these exercises to discover ways to shape your future vision and personal detachment.

After Scott Snider sold his landscaping business, he eventually joined the education company co-owned by his father, The Exit Planning Institute. *"The biggest lesson I learned when selling my first company was, do not let your business define you. One of the reasons I was wandering is because I was "Scott The Landscaper." I didn't realize what I was passionate about was running a business. Whether it's a professional education company, or a landscaping company, it is about the challenge of building and growing a company and working with people and driving great experiences. What I learned over the next ten years is that you need to find your personal purpose."*[16]

Driver 1 - Future Vision Exercises:

1A. Which of the following factors are pushing you to exit your business? Check all that apply.

Personal Readiness to Exit Factors	Major Factor	Minor Factor	Not sure/Not a factor
Concerns about my or a loved one's health			
Burn out			
Family crises			
I'm bored			

Too much stress			
Managing my business takes too much time			
Time to retire			
Market has peaked for my business			
Need to diversify my wealth (minimize risk)			
I need to cash out			
Other			

1B. What are you most excited to spend time on after you exit your business? What are the things pulling you to transition? Check all that apply.

After I exit my business, I want to . . .	Major Factor	Minor Factor	Not sure/Not a factor
Get more involved in philanthropy			
Start or acquire a business			
Focus on my health and get in better shape			
Spend more time with my family			
Spend time on a hobby			

Write a book			
Travel			
Serve on a corporate board			
Get involved in education			
Spend more time with professional communities			
Be a consultant in my industry			
Focus on different income streams or investments (e.g. real estate, day trading)			
Other			

Action Planning: Future Vision and Post-Exit Goals

Use this action planner to add additional details to your post-exit goals regarding your future vision and creating more pull factors.

Using the major and minor factors you identified, write your responses in Table 1C. Prioritize which ones are most interesting to you, and list those first. If you selected "philanthropy" you can detail which organizations, or communities you care about. For "travel," list the countries you want to visit, sights to see, or experiences you would like to have. Provide details about why each is important to you. Lastly, note the approximate timing when you would like these to happen.

Table 1C: Future Vision and Post-Exit Goals

Post-Exit Goal	Details	Why It's Important to Me	Timing

Driver 2 - Personal Detachment Exercises:

2A. Personal Identity—Consider each of the following questions and write the points associated with your responses.

	My Score

a. Hosting a Celebration
If you were to host a big celebration (e.g. wedding, birthday, etc.) who would you invite?
    1. Mostly people from my work (10 points)
    2. Some people from my work (5 points)
    3. No one from my work (0 points)	

b. Starting vs. Inheriting or Buying
Did you start your business?
    1. Yes (10 points)
    2. No (0 points)	

c. Defining Yourself
If you are asked about your work in a social setting, which of the following are you more likely to say?
    1. I am a business owner (10 points)
    2. I own a business (0 points)	

d. How many hours do you put in?
In a typical week, how many hours would you spend working on/in your business?
    1. Less than 30 hours per week (0 points)
    2. 30–39 hours per week (2 points)
    3. 40–49 hours per week (4 points)
    4. 50–59 hours per week (6 points)
    5. 60+ hours per week (10 points)	

e. Is your name on the door?
Is the name of the business associated with you personally such as your initials or last name?
    1. Yes (10 points)
    2. No (0 points)	

Total Score	

Interpreting Your Personal Detachment Score:

Fewer than 20 points: Great! You're separating your personal identity from your business.

20–35 points: Progress! But there's still work to be done.

36+ points: Red Flag! You need to work on your personal detachment.

Starting a business from scratch is a creative process and often becomes an expression of your personal values. Being a founder who started a business (rather than inheriting or acquiring it) can make it harder to separate yourself from your business. Remember that your business is a thing, not a person. While it may have been heavily influenced by you, it is not you.

The next time you are in a social situation, see how long you can keep a conversation going without mentioning your work. This can be harder than it sounds. What are three interesting things about you that you are not directly tied to your business? Focus on being interested in the other person; ask them questions and be curious.

If you are working more than sixty hours a week in your business, consider reducing the hours you spend in your business day-to-day. The more time you spend in the business, the more dramatic the change will feel when you leave.

Consider how you cultivate friendships outside of work. The more you socialize with people from your company, the harder it will be to exit your business without experiencing a sense of isolation and loss.

The longer you've owned your business, the more likely your personal identity and self-worth will become defined by your status as the owner. If you feel a deep connection to your business and a large part of your day-to-day satisfaction is derived from your ties to the entity, consider expanding your interests and accomplishments outside of your work life.

Although your role as the owner or founder of your business likely takes up a lot of time, consider the other roles you play in your life. For example, are you also a parent? Athlete or coach? Volunteer or community leader? List the other roles that you have outside of your work. Take note of your accomplishments in that role and what future goals you have for each area of your life.

2B. Life Roles—Consider what roles and identity you have outside of work.

Make a list of the other roles you play outside of work, what you've accomplished in that role, and your future goals for each area of your life.

Your Role	What You're Proud Of	Future Goals
Parent	8th grade graduation	Ensure child has good transition to high school this year
Sibling	Call sibling each week	See family 4x next year

Spouse	Twenty years of marriage	Celebrate anniversary with a big event, and small things daily
Donor/Giver	Serving on non-profit advisory board	Leading capital campaign this year
Coach	Coaching Little League Team	Make it to regional championship next year

Complete the following table in your own words:

Your Role	What You're Proud Of	Future Goals

2C. Relationships—Consider all of your relationships outside of work.

Make a list of the people you enjoy spending time with outside of work. Note what you appreciate about them. What action will you take this week/month/year to invest in each relationship?

People To Spend Time With Outside of Work	What You Appreciate About Them	Actions You Will Take to Invest in Each Relationship

Sometimes having your name appear in your company name can make it harder to let go. It can be challenging emotionally to separate from your business if your name is on the door.

If you were to exit your company and no longer have control over the governance and operations of the business, how would you feel about the new owner continuing to use your name?

Would you like to see your legacy continue past your tenure or would you feel uncomfortable seeing your family name used in a business you no longer controlled?

If you are in a family business, I encourage you to give significant thought to this question in an exit planning process. You may want to talk with other family members, or if your company has a board of directors (or advisory board) you will want to seek their counsel and alignment as well. Consider what, if any conditions, you would agree to see your family name continue to appear in the company after an exit. This may help you consider who might be the best acquirer or successor to your business, as discussed in Chapter 6.

For founders or family members whose name is on the door of the business (literally or figuratively) there is a strong identity. That identity stems from the community presence you've cultivated, familial and generational pride, employee, and customer relationships.

All these aspects reinforce a business identity, and also your personal identity. It can be a strong pull to stay in the business, to keep it going, to be involved. Could it be that this pull is also holding you back from your future transition?

It's important to be clear about your role when leaving the business. Let me add a perspective to this from my lens as a Mergers and Acquisitions (M&A) advisor.

When I begin a sell-side engagement with a business owner, we talk through a long list of questions to align expectations and path forward. We talk about what they would like their involvement in the business to be post-sale.

Included on this list are questions related to owner transition expectations. For example, I ask, "What role do you want to have with the business after you exit?"

There is no right answer to this question. It is about your preferences, and your vision for achieving a successful exit.

Many times, when owners sell to a third-party, they are usually asked to continue to play a role in the transition of the business to the new owner.

2D. Transition Roles—Consider potential roles in the transition of the business to a new owner.

Which of the options below could be of interest to you? Check all that apply.

Owner Transition Roles	High Interest	Low Interest	Not Sure
I want to exit my company the day I sell my business.			
I am willing to continue to run my company and keep some of my equity in the business for a few years to enjoy a potentially larger exit down the road. (Recapitalization)			
I am willing to be a consultant to the new owner being paid a fixed hourly or daily rate for my time.			
I am willing to continue to run my business for several years after I sell my shares for the opportunity to receive an additional payment, if I achieve a set of future goals agreed upon with the acquirer. (Earnout)			
I am willing to accept part of my sale proceeds over time in the form of a loan to the buyer. (Seller Note)			
I am willing to contemplate a non-compete agreement recognizing this may be a closing condition for the acquirer.			
I am willing to serve on the board of director or board of advisors.			
Other			

The more you've worked on your business and personal readiness for exit, the less reliant the business will be on you. Your offer may include an employment agreement for a relatively short-time-period, or a flexible consulting arrangement focused on areas such as sales, business development, strategic planning, etc.

By working your way through this book, you've been developing your list of transition preferences. Knowing what's important for your personal transition is key. From a buyer's perspective, the more flexibility you have the better. A buyer will ask you about your preferences. You will want to communicate your goals, where you are willing to be more flexible, and what are your non-negotiables.

Owners who are looking to leave the business entirely may prefer 100 percent cash at close, and not want to entertain a consulting agreement or a seller note. Other owners may feel less desire to move on from the business and will be interested in full-time employment with the new owner or in a part-time consulting arrangement.

What Is a Seller Note?

A seller note is a type of debt financing that can serve as an alternative form of business capital. The seller agrees to accept a portion of the purchase price in a series of deferred payments. The purpose of a seller note is to bridge the gap between the purchase price and the financeable asset base of the company being purchased.

It is commonly used in small business acquisitions where the buyer does not have enough cash to pay the entire purchase price upfront. In this scenario, the seller agrees to receive a portion of the purchase price in a series of deferred payments.

This occurs when the business buyer does not have sufficient cash to cover the entire purchase price.

Seller notes are often used when selling a business with challenging characteristics, such as small size, substantial customer concentration, high capital intensity, cyclical nature, or unpredictable revenue patterns.

When a seller note is used, the buyer provides the seller with a written note that outlines the interest rate, repayment terms, and amount owed. Essentially, the seller is self-financing all or part of the transaction.

Seller's notes are quite common in small business transactions since attractive seller financing can lead to a higher selling price than an all-cash deal.

What Is an Earnout?

An earnout is a contractual provision written into purchase agreements stating that the seller of a business will receive additional payments if the business achieves certain financial goals. The earnout eliminates uncertainty for the buyer, as they only pay a portion of the sale price upfront and the remainder based on future performance. The seller receives the benefits of future growth. The differing expectations of a business between a seller and a buyer are usually resolved through an earnout.

While there are different ways to structure an earnout, they are typically stated as a percentage of gross sales or net income. For example, a transaction may be structured with a purchase price of $1 million plus 5 percent of gross sales over the next three years. Earnouts can also be measured on retention of customers or employees. Sometimes there are multiple components of an earnout based on achieving different targets over time.

There are different schools of thought on earnouts. One of my guests on *Succession Stories* is a corporate attorney who developed more than 150 exit plans for business owners over the past decade. In his view, "Your purchase agreement is a report card for the exit and succession planning you've done. When I have an earnout in my purchase price, it means I haven't done the exit plan. Your business has some type of issue, like customer concentration, that's giving the buyer pause. With an earnout the buyer is saying, 'I'm not going to pay you 100 cents on the dollar at closing. I want to make sure everything goes according to plan over the next three years.' That's what we eliminated doing an exit and succession plan. We don't want a haircut in our purchase price at the close."

Succession consultant and author Beth Miller reiterated this point as she recounted her experience as a Vistage Chair with two member companies. It's like if someone wrote a story called "A Tale of Two Successions."

"Obsession With Succession"
Beth Armknect Miller, Executive Velocity Inc.
Succession Stories Podcast E74[17]

"One [owner] *did succession planning successfully and the other didn't. The one that didn't was controlling a lot of what was going on in the business and could never see what life was going to look like after. The group had worked with this individual for about a year saying, "Hey, you're getting older. You need to start planning your succession." But he didn't. He wasn't developing his people like he should. Sadly, I got a call on a Sunday morning that he had died of a heart attack. Eighteen months later that company just shut down. There was nobody prepared to take over the business and it was tragic. The other guy was purposeful about planning for succession and had identified a high potential to take over and had started developing him. At the point when he sold his business, he was only working in the business one day a week. It wasn't a company that needed him, so he got full value upfront. He had no earnout and it was an all-cash deal."*

What Is a Recapitalization?

An equity recapitalization enables you to take some chips off the table. A private investor (individual or private equity group) takes an ownership position in your company while you retain substantial equity in the business. Through this structure, you are creating a financial and strategic partnership with the investors.

Potential benefits of a recapitalization:

- Flexibility—You can seek an investor who is willing to tailor a transaction to meet your personal and financial needs based on how much you want to invest in the business, and how much involvement you want to have in the company going forward.
- Continuity—Investors want your experience, knowledge, and continued passion to grow the business. A recapitalization positions you to stay involved with the company and maintain the culture that you have worked hard to build. Depending on your goals, you can continue in a full-time leadership role with the company or take a step back and contribute as a board member or advisor.
- Liquidity—A recapitalization provides you with liquidity so you can diversify your assets for wealth planning. When designing a transaction, you will want to work with advisors to find the most tax advantaged structure that best suits your needs.
- Equity Appreciation—By maintaining equity in the company, you are positioned for a second bite at the apple. You can reap the rewards of your continued involvement in the business, and by taking the company to the next level with a potential future exit.

---------------------- **TAKE-AWAYS:** ----------------------

- Personal readiness is an important aspect of business transition planning that is often overlooked by business owners.
- It is common for business owners to regret selling their business after the fact and being emotionally unprepared for the transition can lead to feelings of loss and a lack of purpose.
- Prioritizing activities outside of work, such as hobbies, relationships, and charitable endeavors, can help prepare for a successful transition and prevent regrets. It is recommended that business owners dedicate time to these activities in the lead up to a sale or transition.

Consider what you would like your involvement in the business to be after the sale, or whether you are looking to step away completely. Understand your preferences for terms such as an earnout, consulting agreement, seller note, recapitalization, or an employment agreement. If you're interested in completing a Personal Readiness to Exit assessment online, visit www.mytransitionscore.com.

MY ACTION PLAN

What steps will you take to increase your personal exit readiness?

Action Item	Resources Needed	Start By Date	Complete By Date

CHAPTER 5

WHAT DO YOU NEED FINANCIALLY TO EXIT YOUR BUSINESS

If a man knows not to which port he
sails, no wind is favorable.

SENECA

Think back to the reasons you wanted to become a business owner. Maybe you imagined having more freedom in your life compared to having a j-o-b with a boss.

For many entrepreneurs, owning a company puts a constant weight on their shoulders. Demanding customers and employees pull away at your time, money, and ultimately, your happiness.

Selling your business may seem far off into the future. Yet you may decide to exit your business sooner rather than later is to regain a sense of freedom and live a lifestyle you desire.

What if exiting your business now could give you the financial resources to do what you want?

If you engage a business transition advisor like myself, we'll use the exit planning tools and concepts outlined in this book.

Warning: this section requires a pencil and calculator.

Let's estimate whether a transaction would generate enough cash to help you to fund the lifestyle you envision.

What Percentage of Your Net Worth Is Tied To Your Company's Value?

When you launched your business, the company's value was lower than it is today.

Over time, the proportion of your assets tied to your business has likely increased.

Let's imagine a hypothetical business owner named Mike, who starts his company at age thirty-five. Mike has $200,000 of equity in his first home with a $50,000 mortgage, and a small retirement fund of $50,000.

In the beginning, the business does not contribute to Mike's net worth.

Mike's Net Worth:

Assets:	House	$200,000
	Retirement account	$50,000
	Business value	$0
	Total Assets	$250,000
Liabilities:	Mortgage	$50,000
	Student Loan	$20,000
Net Worth:		$180,000

Over the next ten years, Mike invests in his business and follows the value building guidance offered in this book. He has paid off his student loan and has taken on a Small Business Association (SBA) loan for new equipment and a commercial mortgage. He's now forty-five years old.

His net worth picture now looks like this:

Mike's Net Worth:

Assets:	House	$300,000
	Retirement account	$500,000
	Commercial Property	$800,000
	Business value	$3,800,000
	Total Assets	$5,400,000
Liabilities:	Commercial Mortgage	$400,000

Commerical Bank Loan	$50,000
Net Worth:	$4,950,000
Business Value as percent of Net Worth	77%

During the ten-year period, Mike ensured his retirement account followed a diversified investment strategy.

He did not take the same approach with his total net worth picture.

Given the success of his business, it represents 77 percent of Mike's total net worth, while his other assets are around 23 percent.

Understand the Risks for Your Net Worth

Recall the previous chapter about developing your personal exit readiness and a plan for your lifestyle after you exit your business. Maybe you'll travel around the world. Serve on boards. Launch a startup. Buy a business.

After she sold her company, one of my podcast guests said she wanted to be in the "grandparent business" and retire completely. When you have enough money to fund your lifestyle and exit goals, you have reached the freedom point.

What does all of this have to do with business transitions? One word: Risk.

Let's go back to Mike as an example.

With the business representing such a significant piece of his net worth, Mike faces a lot of risk given the lack of total diversification.

It comes down to risk tolerance. The biggest risk Mike faces is a drop in the value of his business.

Recall Bill Prinzivalli. He learned that timing the market for an exit can be risky. Bill rode the growth wave of his business all the way up prior to Y2K, and all the way down as market prospects declined.

"The buyer wants to buy before you reach the big growth cycle because they want to get a return on their investment. If I had gone through that process about two years earlier, I probably would have sold the company. As time kept ticking, the buyers were saying, 'By the time we do this, your Y2K growth spurt will be over. What do you have after that? We don't know if that's going to work.' I feel I was about a year and a half too late."

—Bill Prinzivalli, *Succession Stories Podcast* E111[18]

The 5D's of Business Risk
What Could Cause Business Value to Decline?

There are an infinite number of ways that business value can decline. Identifying potential risk factors is the first step to mitigating those risks.

According to The Exit Planning Institute, 50 percent of exits in the US today are caused by involuntary and unplanned events forcing owners to exit or close their doors.

These are commonly referred to as the 5Ds: Distress, Divorce, Disagreement, Disability, and Death.

DISTRESS: Business distress can be caused by factors that completely disrupt business continuity. These can include natural disasters, outages, and legal issues. The most daunting example of business distress is the global pandemic. While some businesses were emboldened during the crisis, many did not recover to pre-pandemic business value.

Questions to address:

1. What is the strength of your backup system?
2. What insurances do you have to cover business interruption?
3. Do you have contingency plans for everyday disaster situations such as data breaches, property damage, supply chain disruption, safety incidents, and critical employee loss?

DIVORCE: Never a simple process, divorce can be particularly tricky if you and your spouse work in the same business.

Questions to address:

1. How will your shares be valued?
2. Do you have a prenuptial agreement?
3. How will the changes in your finances impact the cash needs of the company?
4. Do you have ways to mitigate the impact on your business?

DISAGREEMENT: You or one of your partners resign from an operational role in your company.

Questions to address:

1. What happens if there is a disagreement between business partners?
2. How can you address conflict?
3. Is there an exit clause?
4. How will your interest be valued?
5. How will you be compensated?

DISABILITY: Something happens to you, making it impossible for you to work. You need to take care of a sick or disabled family member or you are incapacitated.

Questions to address:

1. What will happen if you are forced to exit your business due to your inability to work?
2. If you have a stroke, and cannot read or write, does your family know where your important papers are?
3. Do others have access to essential passwords and accounts that enable them to pay your bills or interact on your behalf?
4. Do you have a power of attorney for financial and medical matters?

5. Would this invoke a purchase of your shares? How will it be paid? Who has the right to vote your shares?

DEATH: It's inevitable. 100 percent of owners will leave their business one day. Will your beneficiaries have to operate a company they do not know how to run? If so, they may likely destroy the value you've created.

Questions to address:

1. What do you want your family, management team, and partners to know?
2. Where will your loans go?
3. What about life insurance and beneficiaries?
4. Who does your team turn to for guidance and direction?
5. Do you have a documented contingency plan for you or your business partner's death?

Recall my client, Don, and his low score on the personal readiness questionnaire in Chapter 2. We were working on an exit plan for his commercial construction company. His son worked in the family business but was exploring other options and had not yet committed to taking over. My client was experiencing stress and the financials of the business were challenging. The business needed improvement, but he never got the chance. He died unexpectedly and did not yet have everything in place for a smooth transition. His wife reached out to ask if his intentions were for his son to own the company. I was glad to relay the conversations I had with Don about his vision and goals to help her decide about what to do with the business.

Assess what you currently have in place to de-risk your business from the negative impacts of these events. Work with advisors to help you with each of these scenarios. Once established, you may want to review on an annual basis to adjust as needed.

Calculate Your Freedom Point

You've reached the freedom point when the net proceeds (after taxes and expenses) of selling your business would generate enough money for you to live comfortably for the rest of your life.

Exit value planning supports the process to find your freedom point, taking measure of the following factors:

- Current business value
- Size of your company
- Amount of debt your business has
- Wealth outside your business (your investments and savings)
- Your timeline
- Your health
- Years in retirement
- Personal financial goals
- How much you need to live comfortably in the future

Recognize that other financial factors play into the numbers as well including:

- Average interest rate you can earn while you are retired
- Average annual inflation rate
- Tax rates

You'll want to talk with a financial planner before making any final decisions. Discuss your situation starting with how much you have saved, what your current investments are, and when you plan to retire.

Also, consider talking with your accountant now about the tax you can expect to pay on the sale of your company in the future. There may be strategies they can recommend to lower your overall tax burden when it comes time to sell.

To calculate when you will have enough value and savings to have the freedom to exit your business, let's walk through the steps:

Step 1: Estimate the income you will need in the future.

Think about where you want to live. Do you want to downsize, travel the world, live on a boat? Estimate how much income you will need annually to feel totally free without financial constraints. It's okay if your number is on the high side. You can reduce it later.

My annual income estimate: _____

Number of years in retirement: _____

Step 2: Calculate your target nest egg

According to Investopedia, the "4 percent Rule"[19] is a way of looking at retirement planning to decide how much you might withdraw each year of your retirement. It provides for a predictable, steady income with the intent to protect you from running short of funds in retirement.

Depending on interest rate conditions, you might choose a withdrawal rate between 3 percent and 5 percent.

For purposes of this exercise, let's be conservative and use a 3 percent withdrawal rate. We'll call it the "3 percent Rule."

Multiply your annual income estimate and years in retirement. This is the nest egg you'll need to finance a long, carefree retirement.

(Annual income) $_____ x (years in retirement) _____ = $_____ target nest egg amount

You also can use online retirement withdrawal calculators, using the 3 percent rule as the amount you intend to withdraw annually.

Step 3: Calculate your wealth outside of your business.

Next step is to estimate the wealth you've created outside of your business. This includes any assets or equities that can be sold relatively easily, such as stocks, bonds, and commercial real estate.

We are not going to include your primary residence in this calculation, because you'll have to live somewhere after you sell your company.

Once you have calculated your assets outside of your business, deduct any debts you have on those assets. Again, be sure to exclude debts on your primary residence or operating business.

Estimated Asset Value:

Number of years in retirement: _____

 Stocks _____

 Bonds _____

 Commercial Real Estate _____

 Other assets _____

 Total assets _____

Estimated Debt Value:

Commercial Mortgage _____

Other debts _____

Total debts _____

Let's say that Mike wants $300,000 in annual income for a forty-year retirement period. That's a nest egg of $12 million outside of his primary residence.

Using the earlier example, Mike has accumulated $900,000 of wealth to-date, including $500,000 from his retirement account, $800,000 for the commercial property, less $400,000 for the commercial mortgage.

He plans to generate $120,000 in annual rent income from his commercial property. Over 40 years, that equals $4.8 million. With these assumptions, his net assets outside the business total $5.7 million.

To reach the freedom point, Mike will need the proceeds from the sale of his company to net at least $6.350 million ($12 million minus $5.7 million) plus $50,000 business debt to be paid. In this example, Mike owns 100 percent of the company.

Step 4: Get an estimate of value for your company.

While you may have heard valuation guidelines in your industry, it's best to check with a professional.

You'll want to work with an M&A advisor to estimate what the shares in your business might be worth to a buyer. In Chapter 7, we will discuss business valuations in more detail.

In our illustration, Mike's business has a 3.8x multiple on $1M EBITDA, resulting in a valuation of $3,800,000.

Step 5: Estimate the costs of selling

There are several expenses to consider when selling your business.

- Taxes on the proceeds of your sale (ordinary income and/or long-term capital gains)
- Legal advisory fees to review and paper your agreements (letter of intent, purchase agreements, etc.)
- Tax accountant advisory fees
- Commission to a business intermediary such as a business broker or M&A professional to sell your company

- In lower middle market transactions, a success fee is a commonly used method for compensating an investment bank or intermediary for arranging a transaction.
- A common method referred to as the "Double Lehman Formula" also called the "Modern Lehman," is calculated as 10 percent of the first million, 8 percent of the second million, 6 percent of the third million, 4 percent of the fourth million, and 2 percent of the remaining transaction value.

While the exact costs of selling your business will vary, here is an example using Mike's transaction value of $3,800,000.

	Percent of Total Transaction Value
M&A Intermediary Commission	8 percent
Legal & Accounting Fees	2 percent
Taxes	20 percent
Estimated total taxes + fees =	30 percent

* Consult your tax advisor for more specific estimates for your business

Add the fees to calculate a gross amount of the transaction:

(Net proceeds needed from sale of the business) x (1 + total percentage %) =$6.35 million x 1.3 = $8.255 million

Step 6: Add any long-term debt on the business

When you sell your business, you'll likely have to pay off any debts and liabilities. To estimate a gross transaction value, you will need to add the amount required to pay back any business loans to the funds you need to reach your freedom point.

In our example with Mike, he has $50,000 of debt in the business.

Step 7: Calculate the potential value gap

This calculation pulls together the three legs of the exit planning stool: personal readiness (knowing what you want to do post-exit and how much it costs), financial readiness (having enough to fund your exit goals), and business attractiveness (making your business attractive, transferable, and sell-ready to achieve your target transaction value). Knowing what your business is worth today and knowing what it needs to sell for in the future are two critical points—if you know these two numbers, and apply a growth rate, we can calculate the time frame to get to this point.

For Mike to achieve his retirement goals, he will need to make his business attractive to buyers to sell for $8.3 million.

With a current valuation of $3.8 million, he's facing a $4.5 million gap.

At forty-five years old, Mike has time to make an impact on his enterprise value through growth and exit value planning.

If the compounded annual growth rate is 8 percent, in this example, Mike would reach his freedom point in ten years, at fifty-five years old.

The Freedom Point Calculator[20]

For illustration purposes only. Assumes you own 100 percent of the company.

Desired Pre-Tax Income		# of Years		Target Nest Egg
$300,000	X	40	=	$ 12,000,000

	Net Amount
Value of your investments or assets not including your primary residence or operating business	$ 1,300,000
Amount of annual income you expect to receive from other sources excluding investments (e.g. guaranteed government income or other guaranteed income sources)	$ 4,800,000

Debt on assets not including your primary residence or operating business	- $ 400,000
Net assets outside of your business	**$ 5,700,000**
Your Gap to Reach The Freedom Point	**= $6,300,000**
Business Long-Term Debt to Be Paid	**+ $ 50,000**
Net Proceeds Needed from Sale of Business	**$ 6,350,000**
M&A Intermediary Commission	8%
Legal & Accounting Fees	2%
Taxes	20%
Total Transactional Cost Estimate Percentage	**+ 30%**
You'll reach the freedom point when your business is worth	**= $8,255,000**
Business valuation estimate	**- $3,800,000**
Potential value gap	**= $4,455,000**

Let's rewind to one of my earlier questions ... do you know what your business is worth?

Knowing the answer can inform risks you might face if your business represents a big slice of your net worth.

Determine the net number that would fund your future lifestyle. Write this number down. Seal it in an envelope and put it in a drawer. That's your walk-away target.

A business owner who knows how much they need for exit, how much the business is worth today, and has a clear idea of the current growth rate, can begin the process of exit planning by knowing their freedom point.

Knowing the gross value of your business is only one part of the formula. If you sell your business, your net number is after taxes and professional fees. Compare this to the number we've calculated for what you need for your future. Does this motivate you to eliminate the gap, if there is one, so you are on a successful path forward?

"Clearing Blurred Lines of Business Transition" Chris Chaney, Vice President, Fort Pitt Capital Group Succession Stories Podcast E22[21]

Chris Chaney is a vice president at Fort Pitt Capital, an investment advisory firm serving clients across the US. We discussed the challenge that for almost every owner, their business is about 80 percent of their financial wealth. Recognizing potential risks is important to avoid larger problems down the road.

"I remember talking to an owner who was very comfortable with his business. He knew it inside and out. When you're directly involved, and you can take action, you feel like you've got more control. Making decisions gives you that feeling of control.

If I told you that you were to take all your money and put it into one extremely small illiquid stock, would you feel comfortable? Would you feel like you weren't taking too much risk? This is a very illiquid stock. It's very subject to the whims and the vagaries of the local economy. Would you do that?

But that's what you've done. You may feel like you've got control because you're involved day-to-day. Let's look at your business. This may well be the most successful investment you ever have, but I've got to make sure that all the elements of your financial picture are working together for you. If we encounter a change in your financial fortunes or the fortunes of the business, which again, may largely be beyond your control that you're protected and your family's protected.

More importantly, it reduces the stress that you're going to experience when we go through that.

We can have tremendous stresses on the business. Most owners are trying to get liquidity and make sure they've got adequate cash reserves. Part of my job is to make sure that we're building financial buffers. If we can take pressure off of the business owner, then we will have one less stress, which allows them to focus more freely and more productively on the challenges of the business. I look at their whole financial plan."

TAKE-AWAYS:

- There are many reasons why a business can increase or decrease in value.
- Every one of us is going to leave our business one day. The five D's of business transition can derail the business if you're not prepared.
- Understand whether your business makes up most of your net worth. If you sold the business, would the net amount enable you to live carefree for the rest of your life?
- At what point does the risk of owning the business outweigh the benefits? Looking strictly at the numbers, keeping it may be unnecessarily risky for your future.

MY ACTION PLAN:

How will you determine what you need financially to exit your business?

Action Item	Resources Needed	Start By Date	Complete By Date

CHAPTER 6

WHO SHOULD OWN YOUR BUSINESS AFTER YOU

If you don't know where you are going,
you will end up somewhere else.

YOGI BERRA

Considering that all owners will leave their companies one day, it's only natural that I ask who should own your business after you?

When it comes to potential buyers, there are three main categories: strategic buyers, financial buyers, and related buyers.

A framework to consider is the 5–20 Rule.

The 5–20 Rule

To think about who an acquirer might be for your business, consider the "5–20 Rule"—a general rule espoused by entrepreneur and author, John Warrillow. John is the best-selling author of the books *Built to Sell, The Automatic Customer*, and *The Art of Selling Your Company*, and he's the founder of The Value Builder System™.

In simplest terms, the 5–20 Rule suggests that a likely buyer is between five and twenty times your size.

Let's break it down. Say your business is doing $5 million in top-line revenue. With a 5–20 Rule mindset, a potential acquirer would have a top-line of at least $25 million (5x) and no more than $100 million (20x).

What's the reason behind this approach? If the acquirer is not at least five times as large as you, there may be more issues and risks on both sides.

For example, if the companies face challenges and the acquisition fails over time, you run a greater chance that both businesses would not survive. For a much larger business, a failed acquisition write-off may have a smaller impact on the acquirer's profit and loss (P&L) statement.

Another reason is because you may be less likely to get the attention of a company more than twenty times your size. The acquisition is probably too immaterial for the acquirer.

That said, the 5–20 Rule is not written in stone. There are exceptions to the rule with acquisitions from Facebook and Google. These deals are less common in non-tech sectors like services, industrial, hospitality, consumer products, and retail.

Could it happen? Think of it as Goliath acquiring David. Is there something your company has that a billion-dollar company can't easily replicate? What would be the path of least resistance for the buyer to achieve that goal? The likelihood of a billion-dollar company acquiring your company is slim, but then again, crazier things have happened.

Strategic Buyers

Strategic buyers are operating companies with a goal to acquire companies whose products or services can integrate with their existing P&L to create incremental, long-term value for owners and stakeholders.

These buyers can also be unrelated to your company and looking to grow in your market to diversify their revenue sources. Strategic buyers can be a publicly traded or privately held company.

The industry in which a business operates will also have differing importance based on the buyer type. Since strategic acquirers are usually wedded to a general industry, by nature of their core products and services, they will spend a great deal of time focusing on how your business can integrate with their overall corporate strategy. Very often, these strategic buyers are looking to acquire a company that can quickly and clearly impact the bottom line.

In the value chain, they could be more upstream or downstream to your company. Likely there is an aspect of the business that is related and synergistic with your business. They could be an existing partner, supplier, or customer of your firm, or even a competitor.

For industries that are highly regulated, unpredictable, or discretionary, pursuing relationships with a strategic buyer can help mitigate the risks associated with an industry.

If an established businesses wants to achieve at least 10 percent growth annually, perhaps they can get 5 percent growth organically. They may invest in more marketing or sales resources, launch new products, or expand their geographic footprint. To get the additional 5 percent annual revenue boost, they may decide to pursue acquisitions.

Strategic buyers seek accretive acquisitions. An accretive acquisition occurs when the value of the buyer increases because of acquiring a specific company. If the buyer is valued at a higher enterprise value than the acquired company, the buyer's multiple gets applied to the combined entity's EBITDA, essentially resulting in multiple arbitrages on the acquisition.

To realize the forecasted results, strategic buyers can implement different strategies to create "synergy." This process includes optimizing the balance sheet and reducing interest expense, removing redundant operating expenses and headcount, or increasing top-line revenue through cross-selling. The key to having an accretive acquisition is the ability to successfully integrate both companies.

Let's also consider reasons why strategic buyers pursue acquisitions.

- **Speculating**
  When a company acquires a smaller company that has a new product or solution for potential growth opportunities in the future. A great example of a speculative acquisition is when Facebook (now known as Meta Platforms) acquired the messaging service WhatsApp in 2014. The original agreement, made in February 2014, was for $19 billion, primarily in the form of Facebook stock. The stock shot up in the subsequent months, and when the deal closed in October 2014, the actual price was $21.8 billion. All for a company that lost $138 million on $10 million of sales.

Facebook also bought Instagram on speculation. The company paid $1 billion in 2012. At the time, this was a shocking amount for a company with thirteen employees. Instagram reached two billion active users and contributed over $47 billion to Meta's annual revenue in 2021. Instagram was responsible for 44 percent of Meta Platforms revenue in 2021 and is expected to surpass Facebook as Meta's main revenue source in 2024.[22]

- **Value Creating**

  A company acquires another company to improve the purchased company's performance. DropBox acquired HelloSign, an e-signature platform, to fulfill their strategy to provide a digital hub for organizations. Google's purchase of Android to turbocharged development and help turn it into the dominant smartphone operating system.

- **Consolidating**

  A company acquires another company to remove the excess capacity in the industry. Walmart bought Flipkart for $16B to remove crowded competition in the online market.

- **Resource Acquiring**

  This is a faster and easier way to gain skills, market position, or technology than develop internally. Apple bought Siri to enhance the iPhone experience and bought Beats because the music streaming market was shifting away from purchasing and downloading iTunes music.

  Team acquisitions (also known as an "Acqui-Hire" strategy) can be a primary motivator for an acquirer to improve the level of their team's talent in certain skill areas. Additionally, the management team may provide a deeper bench and succession strategy for the acquiring company.

- **Accelerating**

  A company acquires another company to accelerate growth and increase market share. It works often when the acquired company has loyal customers, and the industry is very competitive, so the acquirer highly benefits from the acquisition. Microsoft acquired LinkedIn for $26 billion in 2016 (7.2x revenue).

- **Asset Acquisitions**

  Should a company invest the time and money to build out a new product or enter a new segment of the market? Or would an asset acquisition enable them to leapfrog their current roadmap? How would an acquisition increase the customer base, top-line revenue, and future growth opportunities? For some companies, it makes sense to acquire certain assets such as products, technology, or intellectual property. The buyer can continue to operate as a stand-alone product or choose to integrate into their product suite.

A strategic acquisition can dramatically impact the acquirer's business opportunities by a significant multiple. The opportunities a strategic acquisition opens for an acquirer include, but are not limited to:

- Market consolidation
- Ability to cross-sell
- Opportunity to enter a new market
- Ability to hinder a current or potential competitor's market positioning

Financial Buyers

Financial buyers include private equity firms, family offices, and high net worth individuals. These firms and executives are in the business of making investments in companies and realizing a return on their investments within five to seven years with a sale or an Initial Public Offering (IPO).

Private equity describes investment partnerships that buy and manage companies before selling them. PEGs raise capital from limited partners and managing partners determine how to invest those funds. Private equity firms operate these investment funds on behalf of institutional and accredited investors. Investors in this asset class are usually required to commit significant capital for years, which is why access to such investments is generally limited to institutions and individuals with high net worth.

What Is a Leveraged Buyout (LBO)?

An LBO is the acquisition of a company, either privately held or publicly traded, where a significant amount of the purchase price is funded using debt. The remaining portion is funded with equity contributed by the financial sponsor and in some cases, equity rolled over by the company's existing management team.

Once the transaction closes, the acquired company will have undergone a recapitalization and transformed into a highly leveraged financial structure.

The sponsor will typically hold onto the investment between five and seven years. According to Private Equity Info, the average holding period for a private equity portfolio company was about five years in 2021.

Throughout the holding period, the acquired company will use the cash flows that it generates from its operations to service the required interest payments and pay down some of the debt principal.

The financial sponsor will usually target an IRR investment rate of return, of approximately 20–25 percent.

The fund has a time horizon on it, and they might do hybrid deals. In many cases, a strategic buyer will value the business higher than a financial buyer.

The investment horizon for a financial acquirer in the context of the overall business cycle will have an important impact on the return on their invested capital.

Let's say a private equity firm acquires a company at the peak of a business cycle for 8X EBITDA. If five years later, they can only sell it for 6X EBITDA, it will be difficult to achieve a return on their investment. Given the shorter time-horizons, financial buyers can be more sensitive to business cycle risk than strategic buyers. In the deal evaluation process, they will consider various exit strategies for your business before making a final decision to acquire your company.

While the 5–20 Rule is sound logic for strategic buyers, don't be surprised if private equity groups operate outside those boundaries. Private Equity Groups are becoming more aggressive and increasingly strategic as they continue to do add-on acquisitions for their portfolio companies.

Before an LBO can occur, the sponsor must first secure the necessary financing commitments from financial institutions such as corporate banks and specialty lenders.

The financial sponsor must convince the lenders that the prospective LBO target can handle the post-LBO debt load to raise the amount of financing needed to fund the transaction.

To protect their downside risk and potential for capital loss, lenders must be adequately assured that the borrower (i.e. the LBO target) is unlikely to default on its financial obligations.

How Do Private Equity Groups Create Value?

When a private equity firm acquires a company, it has a plan to increase the investment's worth. That could include dramatic cost cuts or restructuring, steps the company's incumbent management may have been reluctant to take. PEGs with a limited time to add value before exiting an investment have more of an incentive to make major changes.

The private equity firm may also have special expertise the company's prior management lacked. It may help the company develop an e-commerce strategy, adopt new technology, or enter additional markets. A private equity firm acquiring a company may bring in its own management team to pursue such initiatives or retain prior managers to execute an agreed-upon plan.

What Is an Add-On Acquisition?

An add-on acquisition in private equity refers to the purchase of a smaller-sized target by an existing portfolio company, where the acquired company is integrated into the existing portfolio company.

The strategy of add-on acquisitions (also known as buy-and-build) has become more common in the private equity industry.

Under such a strategy, after the initial buyout of the core portfolio company—often referred to as the "platform"—the financial sponsor seeks to create value by acquiring smaller-sized targets and integrating them accordingly. If a financial buyer already owns a company in your space and is looking to make strategic add-ons, it is likely they will evaluate your business more like a strategic buyer.

How Do Private Equity Firms Exit Yheir Investment?

The most common ways for a private equity firm to monetize its investment are:

Sale to a Strategic Buyer
A sale to a strategic buyer tends to be the most convenient and lucrative. Strategic buyers tend to be willing to pay a premium for potential synergies.

Secondary Buyout (aka Sponsor-to-Sponsor Deal)
Another option is the sale to another financial buyer. For a PEG, this is a less than ideal exit as financial buyers cannot pay a premium for synergies.

Initial Public Offering (IPO)
The third method for a private equity firm to monetize its profits is for the portfolio company to undergo an IPO and sell its

shares in the public market—however, this is only an option for big firms.

What attributes make a business an ideal LBO candidate?

Certain industries attract more interest from private equity investors. These tend to be mature, non-cyclical industries with moderate growth rates and positive economic tailwinds. Companies in these industries are more likely to generate predictable revenue with fewer disruption risks from technological advancements or new entrants due to having high barriers to entry. Examples of companies include energy, transportation, and telecommunications.

If the investment strategy of the firm is based around roll-up acquisitions, the private equity firm will look for fragmented industries where a consolidation strategy (buy-and-build) is more viable with potential add-on targets in the market.

There are exceptions, but management wanting to rollover a portion of their equity to participate in the potential upside is perceived as a positive signal to PE investors. The willingness of management to rollover equity is proof of their confidence in actual value creation opportunities, as pitched in the sale process of the company.

An ideal LBO candidate should have most (or all) of the following characteristics:[23]

- Steady, predictable free cash flow
- Operates in a mature industry with defensible market position
- Recurring revenue with non-cyclical performance
- Diversified revenue streams with minimal cyclicality
- Favorable unit economics and high margins
- Strong, committed management team (rollover equity)
- Low capital expenditure and low working capital requirements
- Low purchase price multiple (undervalued acquisition target)

The quality of a company's cash flows is a function of its predictability and defensibility—as well as the certainty of occurrence with minimal risks.

Private equity firms seek product or service offerings that fit their fund strategy, including industry focus, firm-specific criteria, and the specific post-LBO strategies employed.

Several product or service attributes are commonly found across almost all LBO targets. There are several recurring themes that make certain industries more appealing to private equity firms:

Mission Critical: The ideal product/service is essential to the end market being served. If customers no longer had access, it would be detrimental to business continuity, result in severe monetary consequences, or reputational damage.

For example, the decision for a data center to terminate its contract with its security solutions provider (e.g. video surveillance, access control) could impair the data center's relationships with its existing customers in the case of a security breach and loss of confidential customer data.

Non-Cyclical: Industries that are non-cyclical (or "defensive") are stable regardless of the economic conditions, which makes their financial performance more predictable and less of a liability, particularly to lenders.

Low-Growth: Most industries with high LBO deal flow are anticipated to exhibit low to moderate growth in the coming years, as that tends to coincide with minimal disruption risk and more stability—but there are numerous exceptions, such as B2B enterprise software (which is higher growth but still attractive to PE firms as LBO targets).

Fragmented: If an industry is fragmented, that means that competition is local (or regional), rather than in a "winner-takes-all" industry, which reduces the risk to all companies operating in the industry as well as creates more opportunities for PE firms that specialize in add-on acquisitions and rely on inorganic growth (i.e. location-based competition).

Contractual (or Subscription-Based) Revenue: Not all revenue is created equally, as contractual and subscription-based revenue cause a company's cash flows to be of "higher" quality, i.e., more recurring revenue with greater predictability relative to one-time purchases. Products or services that require maintenance and have a recurring revenue component are more valuable given the greater predictability in revenue. In most cases, customers prefer to receive maintenance and other types of related services from the original provider they purchased the product from.

High Research & Development Spend: The more technical a product (and R&D expenditures) the fewer competitors there are, which reduces external threats given the technical barrier that deters competitors—plus, the benefits of pricing power from establishing an R&D-oriented niche and the absence of competition.

Synergistic Integrations: Certain industries are prone to "roll-ups," as there are more opportunities for synergies to be realized, which can come in the form of revenue synergies (e.g., upselling, cross-selling, product bundling), as well as cost synergies (e.g., economies of scale, economies of scope, cost-cutting areas, upgrading outdated technology, improving inefficient cost structure).

Favorable Industry Trends: Industries positioned well to benefit from long-term structural shifts and ongoing tailwinds are more likely to be targeted by PE firms, as optimism surrounding an industry tends to warrant higher multiples later, especially if add-on acquisitions increase technical capabilities and scale.

High Switching Costs: The decision to switch to another provider should come with high costs that make customers reluctant to move to a competitor. Switching costs should outweigh the benefits of moving to a lower-cost provider.

With more than 4,500 private equity firms in the US alone, it is possible to target potential PEGs based on industry focus and matching to their investment criteria to find the right fit for your business.

PEGs have committed equity capital. PE investors (limited partners) make binding, legal commitments to fund acquisitions. When PEGs find an attractive acquisition candidate, they can invest in that company without outside approval.

Family Offices

Family offices are another type of financial buyer. In the United States there are between 15,000 and 30,000 family offices with $3 trillion dollars to invest. These investors may have generational wealth or have sold real estate or businesses. Family offices develop an investment thesis to invest and or acquire businesses through their direct efforts. Many see direct investment as a way to tap into the entrepreneurial DNA that made the family business successful.

Family office investors are somewhat like a private equity group, but they're not investing third-party money from investors. They are investing their own money from the family.

One of the key advantages to working with family office investors is that they have a longer time horizon than private equity groups, potentially holding the asset in perpetuity. That's why family office investments are commonly referred to as "patient capital."

"Launching a Family Office"
Alex Panosian, CW Growth Partners
Succession Stories Podcast E73[24]

Laurie Barkman:
PE funds are known to have more of a foreseeable exit time horizon, call it five to seven years. They've set that exit timeline early on, and it's known to all par-

ties that's the plan. Is that different in a family office? Will family offices target companies for a longer time horizon because they are looking for this promise to generate value over a mid- to long-term without a preset expiration date?

Alex Panosian:
Certainly, every family office is different. The joke goes, if you talk to thirty different family offices, you'll probably get thirty different answers. I think one thing that separates family offices from the other private equity groups, or some of the other types of buyers, is they don't always have investors. They may bring other folks in on a deal. Generally, they don't have investors that they're going to be beholden to because they're using their own capital. That gives them the opportunity to be flexible on things like time-horizons, trend transitions, structure, and they can really tailor it to what the business owner wants.

The most important question that we're going to ask a business owner is, "What are your goals?" So we can understand and start to talk about that. I think where we're a good fit is another family-owned business, that for whatever reason, maybe doesn't have the next generation lined up. Or almost in a sense recognizes the value and care about the legacy. They really care about their employees, their customers, and they want to make sure that all those different stakeholders are treated in the right way.

Why we're a good fit there is because we don't have to sell it in three to five years. Frankly, we don't want to. My dad has never sold a business but has bought four. We still hope to own those for the next thirty years and beyond. That influences the type of business that we're going to target, of course. That's how structurally we're a little bit different than some of the other buyers out there.

Laurie Barkman:
What do you look for in an acquisition?

Alex Panosian:

We have a geographic filter, so we look predominantly in the Midwest. I'm in Chicago, my dad is in Milwaukee, so we look heavily in those markets. Then size wise, we look at the smaller end of what you can label as the lower middle market so around $2 million in bottom line, and then we're going to look for stability through a transition, and then growth potential thereafter. For stability through a transition, we're really going to look for quality of revenues, so whether there'll be some aspect of recurring revenues, or contracted revenues, or very high percentage of repeat business, that's important for us, because it's going to give us the confidence that we can carry that revenue through. I think one of the challenges, certainly, for a lot of business owners to think about is, a lot of businesses in this size are reliant on the owners. Well, that's natural, and that's great while you're running the business, but it becomes hard to sell the business in that case. That's something that we really dive into. Then the other thing that we're going to at the situation and why it makes sense for us, and the seller to work with us, versus going through a private equity group.

One of our value-adds is boosting up the management team. That doesn't mean investing cash flows in additional management team members if there's a CEO or a general manager in place. If we must replace them that would be in the plan. We can bring in peers of mine, talented people who desire to work in a small business and help them grow these companies going forward.

Laurie Barkman:

It was interesting to hear about this because ultimately, if a seller wants to maximize their opportunity, or they want to really understand which value drivers are important to which buyers. That's something that I advocate for in terms of the process that I use. We are essentially providing some of that insight right now. You're giving a great example by sharing what some of your deal criteria are: the size, the geography, the stability through the transition. Do you look for an owner to stay on for a certain period and how long?

Alex Panosian:

Generally, we're going to hope that the owner stays on through the transition. That can mean different things in many different scenarios. A lot of it is going to be dependent on how active the owner is in the business today. We've looked at everything across the spectrum. We've talked to companies where the owner is not involved at all anymore, and they've hired a general manager. At that point, it's clearly not as important. Then we've looked at other businesses where the owner is the only person in the entire company that talks to customers, and so they have every customer relationship. It's hard to buy a business like that because it's very difficult to separate the owner from the business. In a scenario like that, we're going to want a longer transition, maybe twelve, even twenty-four months.

In some situations, we're going to want to make sure that we're aligned. From both the future strategy that we want to take, and that everyone is incentivized. If they're going to help hand off those lessons, they would benefit from a little bit of the upside. There is another thing that we found that's maybe a little bit different than some other buyers. We certainly come in with ideas. But at the same time, we're appreciative of long-term expertise in an industry. We'd be a little bit silly if we didn't try to grab all the great ideas the current ownership has. We have a lot of conversations where the owner's like, "If I just had three young, hungry people to help me go after these things, I would do this, this, and this. But I'm just tired, and I want to retire." Let's grab those ideas, and we can help you implement those types of things.

Acquisition Entrepreneurs

Entrepreneurship Through Acquisition (ETA) is the path to becoming an entrepreneur by buying and growing an established small business. For individuals with business skills and a desire to make a meaningful impact, this can be less risky than starting a new business around an unproven product or service.

ETA is typically pursued later in a person's professional life after they gain operational experience and a more robust professional network. Over the past two decades, ETA has become a more recognized career path.

ETA is the beneficiary of a major demographic trend in the United States: more than 40 percent of all small businesses are owned by "baby boomers" - people over age 60. All baby boomer business owners need management succession and ownership transition. A survey by Wilmington Trust suggests that nearly 60 percent of boomers do not have a succession plan.[25]

An acquisition entrepreneur is typically a self-funded or sponsored sole investor who will run the business directly as the operator. Or they seek to acquire the business as part of a larger strategy to develop a holding company of smaller businesses.

A fundless sponsor is a group or individual seeking to identify acquisition candidates and negotiate acquisitions without having the equity financing in place to complete the transaction.

A search fund is a group or individual that has raised a small amount of capital from investors to search for an acquisition target. They identify and negotiate a transaction with a target and then the investors will receive an option to invest in the target company, or pass, as they see fit.

Small business and ETA go together because there are a lot of small businesses in need of ownership transition and management succession and the capital required to acquire a small business is lower.

Characteristics of an ideal ETA acquisition target:

- Mature business—minimum ten-year operating history
- $1.5M to $15M annual revenue
- Good profit margins—Minimum 15–20 percent EBITDA margin (EBITDA/Sales)
- Outstanding reputation and brand
- Loyal customers / recurring revenue
- Pricing and location advantage

Ron Skelton, acquisition entrepreneur, and host of the *How2Exit Podcast*, offers these additional criteria:

- Fragmented industry—lots of small and medium firms
- Less competition
- Low debt
- Able to cross-sell in portfolio
- Can scale without heavy reliance on more employees
- Low outside investment
- Buyers available (PEGs and holding companies buying)
- Industry not primed to be disrupted before business is sold in future
- No single party can disrupt the business
- Low capital requirements to grow
- Face minimal expensive or regulatory issues
- See a path to scale or grow the business

The self-funded search, often referred to as a "fundless sponsor," is when an individual looks for or "sponsors" an acquisition without the "funds" anticipating third-party funding will be secured.

The entrepreneur bears all the costs to find a suitable acquisition target. Once a business is identified, the entrepreneur determines the best funding strategy for the acquisition.

Deals are funded by a combination of personal funds, investor capital, seller financing, and bank financing. Keep in mind—nearly all small business acquisitions start as self-funded searches.

"Acquisition Entrepreneur Buy-Side Deals"
Ron Skelton, How2Exit
Succession Stories Podcast E93[26]

What do acquisition entrepreneurs look for in buy-side deals? Serial entrepreneur and investor Ron Skelton shared his approach to buying existing small to medium sized businesses. Ron discussed his deal criteria, how buyers are different, and the importance of having a transferable business when you're ready to sell.

"It's not an overnight process. You decide to sell your business today, we're going to look at your last three years' track record. Tax returns, financials, bank statements for the business to give us a longer-term view. A view of where you've been and where you're going. You can't just start packaging up today and slightly decide to sell unless you've been running well for the last couple of years.

I always thought people sold to the highest and best offer. I would say more than probably 80 percent of these deals don't go that route. They're looking for the safest pair of hands. Understand what you want in your buyer. If you think it's money, when you get down to it toward the end, you'll figure out that it's not so much the money. The money will probably be close between the top two or three potential buyers. But there are things out there that you're going to want more than money."

Related Buyers

A related buyer might literally be related to you as family. Or they could be management or one partner buying out the other partner. Below are some examples.

Family Succession

You may be surprised to learn that only a third of family business organizations have a robust, documented, and communicated succession plan in place.[27]

If you want to transition the leadership and ownership of your business to family members, take the time to work out a plan.

There is a saying "from shirt sleeves to shirt sleeves in three generations." The first generation takes the entrepreneurial risk, starting with little and building up wealth to pass along. The second generation preserves the wealth, generally by keeping status quo or not taking chances. The third generation spends it all, missing the opportunity to bring the business back to its prior level, and the family returns to having very little.

It is possible to break this cycle. In my conversations with multi-generation companies, here are common themes I've noted from stories of next generation success:

- Desire—the next generation wants to work in the business and the decision is 100 percent theirs. They are not forced to do so.
- Fit—just like any other new hire, the next gen candidate needs to be the right fit for the role, and the company.
- Value—next gen leaders make an impact by driving measurable or highly visible results.
- Mentorship—next gen leaders benefit by having mentors and by being coachable.
- Humility—they recognize and appreciate how they are part of something larger than themselves.

Laird & Company is the oldest commercial distillery and the twenty-sixth-oldest family business in the United States. With an official founding date of 1780, the company history of apple brandy production stretches back to colonial times and George Washington.

Lisa Laird Dunn, executive vice president, is the ninth generation, and her son, Gerard Dunn is the tenth generation Laird to join the family business. "My position is operations manager. I do a little bit of everything, still trying to learn from everyone in the company. I first started working here when I was fourteen years old in the summer just to gain a little bit of extra cash. It led to me being fully interested in the business, and here I am. Probably half our employees were here when I first started when I was fourteen years old. I grew up with them. Everyone here has mentored me in some way. Growing up in that type of environment is definitely something that I cherished and realized how lucky I was."

There is more discussion on family succession in Chapter 12.

"NextGen Growth By Acquisition"
Ben Grossman, Co-President
Grossman Marketing Group
Succession Stories Podcast E64[28]

Ben Grossman is the co-president of the Grossman Marketing Group, a fourth-generation business he has co-led with his brother for more than ten years.

"One of the best pieces of advice I got was to find a way to generate revenue as quickly as possible, because no one can ever question your existence at an organization if you're generating revenue. That's certainly a challenge that NextGen family business members face. When they join a family business, people are watching them. They have sort of an X on their back. Make sure that NextGen is not going to put their feet up on their desk and collect a paycheck. What are they going to do to better those around them in terms of more job security, and helping pave a clear path to the future? Hard numbers speak for themselves and try to find a way to generate revenue.

Another piece of advice I got was come in and be humble. Put your head down, learn, become an expert in the business, so when you speak, you are right. Sometimes the next generation in family businesses can come into an organization without much of a filter and reference materials that they learned in business school or other organizations. That doesn't necessarily mean it's appropriate or applicable to that specific company that has been around for quite some time.

I took a lot of time to immerse myself in the company, to make sure that I knew what I was talking about, and when I spoke, I was right. Between finding ways to generate revenue, learning the business, and trying to comport myself in a humble manner, which I try to do all the time anyway, but I was extra mindful of how I would be perceived coming into a fourth-generation business. Several colleagues had known me since I was a kid, and some have even been around with the company since before I was born. I was very cognizant of the image that I communicated to my colleagues."

Management Buyout

A management buyout (MBO) is when a company's existing leadership team purchases either 100 percent of the business from the shareholders or a majority stake (greater than 51 percent of the company's voting shares). In most cases, the management team takes full control and ownership of the business, and the prior owners retire or move on to other ventures.

In 2013, Michael Dell partnered with a private equity firm to purchase the computer company he founded from shareholders. He took Dell private before the company went public again in 2018.

Like a leveraged buyout, an MBO transaction typically involves external financing. The company is purchased using a combination of debt and equity, and the cash flow of the business is the collateral used to secure and repay the loan.

An MBO enables you to transition your ownership in your business to your management team. If you have been developing your management team, and they are interested in ownership, this may be a succession option to consider.

More details on internal transactions with management are covered in Chapter 12.

Employee Stock Ownership Plans

An Employee Stock Ownership Plan (ESOP) is an opportunity for succession planning whereby you sell your business to a trust. An ESOP is a tax-qualified retirement plan authorized and encouraged by federal tax and pension laws.

Currently, there are around 7,000 ESOP plans in the US with estimates that 28 million employees now control about 8 percent of corporate equity through an ESOP.[29]

An ESOP allows you to remain as CEO and actively manage the business, even if you've sold a minority equity stake.

For the right company, an ESOP can be an effective way to facilitate succession planning. In doing so, you provide employees with a wealth creation vehicle that rewards their service, and that also maintains your legacy.

There are significant tax benefits that go with selling to an ESOP. If you're a C Corp, you can defer capital gains if you sell to the ESOP trust. If you're an S Corp, you pay no federal or state income taxes for the part of the business that is owned by the ESOP trust.

Kristy Britsch is a corporate attorney advising closely held businesses on ESOP transactions throughout their life cycle. "When you're forming an ESOP it's just like any other M&A transaction, so it's not any more expensive. Any owner that's ever gone through an acquisition, whether they purchased a company or whether their company may have been purchased, at some point, the ESOP transaction is going to operate that same way. The only difference is the person buying your stock is an employee stock ownership trust. An outside independent trustee is an ERISA fiduciary, and their goal is to make sure that the ESOP trust that's buying the stock from the owner is not paying more than fair market value."[30]

The Employee Retirement Income Security Act of 1974 is a U.S. federal tax and labor law that establishes minimum standards for pension plans in private industry. It contains rules on the federal income tax effects of transactions associated with employee benefit plans.

According to the ESOP Association, several advantages of the ESOP structure include:

Common Sense Succession Planning
Sell your business to the people who care most about your legacy—the employees.

Sell on Your Timeline
Unlike a sale or merger, the ESOP enables you to sell any portion of the company you choose. A sale or merger usually requires the seller to sell a controlling stake of the business.

Liquidity
An ESOP is a ready buyer of company shares.

1042 Rollover
If the ESOP acquires 30 percent or more of the outstanding stock of a privately held company, any capital gains on the transaction can be deferred indefinitely.

Tax Deductible
Repay debt with tax deductible or tax-free dollars.

Productivity
Because employee owners have a stake in the business, they work harder and smarter.

Profitability
ESOP companies are often more profitable than their peers and more likely to withstand financial hardships like a pandemic.

There are annual requirements to maintain an ESOP. There are ESOP advisory firms and attorneys who can help you understand whether your company qualifies, and how an ESOP would benefit you. A business that is at least $1 million to $2 million in EBITDA might consider this option. Common industries for ESOPs including construction, engineering, and manufacturing.

If you want to explore an ESOP for your business, I encourage you to speak with advisors who specialize in ESOPs from a tax and legal perspective.

Summary: Which Buyer Is Right for You?

In the private market, buyers determine the value. In the public market, we can look up the value of the company on the web. But in the private market, the value is in the eye of the buyer.

When we consider who might buy our company, we're talking about transfer channel options: the different types of buyers and investors, their motives, what sources of capital are available to them, and the types of transactions that can be done. For the different types of investors, they have different motives and then they have different ways to value a business.

Financial buyers may desire the management team to stay intact because they may not have operators sitting on the sidelines ready to jump in. In these instances, they might want you to stay on to support the transition and then exit.

The take-away is that there will likely be a wide range differences between buyer motivations and post-integration vision. This only under-scores the importance of clearly knowing your goals; this clarity will allow you to pursue exit options that make the most sense for you. Because these buyers have fundamentally different goals, the way they approach your business in a M&A sale process can differ in significant ways.

Buyers have different motivations for buying a company. A strategic buyer might be more interested in the assets of your business: your cus-tomer list, technology, know-how, and employee talent. If it's a competitor interested in consolidation, they might not be interested in the goodwill or the brand name of your business. In acquiring your company, a stra-tegic buyer might have a duplication of roles—often back-office roles like accounting, human resources, and IT—that may be consolidated post-acquisition.

One of the most significant differences between strategic and finan-cial acquirers is how they evaluate your business. Strategic buyers focus heavily on synergies and integration capabilities, while financial buyers look at standalone cash-generating capability and the capacity for earn-ings growth.

There are a wide range of ways to handle transactions. Most commonly in the lower middle market, a buyer will acquire 100 percent of the company or a majority stake. If you want to take some chips off the table you could sell a minority stake (49 percent or less) of voting shares. You could choose to stay operational in the business or take a step back and serve as an advisor or expert when needed.

Key Differences Between Strategic and Financial Buyers

	Strategic Buyers	Financial Buyers
Evaluation of Your Business	Focus heavily on synergies and integration capabilities. Critical to consider how the target will fit with their existing company and business units.	Look at stand-alone cash-generating capability and the capacity for earnings growth. Often acquired as a stand-alone entity.
Integration Strategy	Typically incorporate the acquired business into a larger business.	PEG platform deals are typically operated as stand-alone entities and not integrated into a larger company. PEG add-ons or tuck-ins are integrated into platform entities in the portfolio.
Investment Horizon	"Infinite Holding Period" Strategics plan to keep a newly purchased business indefinitely, often fully integrating the company into their existing business.	"Finite Holding Period" Private Equity Groups have an investment time horizon of only five to seven years. Family Offices tend to have a longer time horizon, more like strategics.

Industry Focus	Focus on industry of their core product/ services to clearly impact the bottom line.	Not wedded to a single industry. Evaluating the attractiveness of a specific business and the attractiveness of the broader industry.
Back-Office Infrastructure	May focus less on the strength of the target company's existing "back-office" infrastructure (IT, HR, Payables, Legal, etc.) Will evaluate which functions may be redundant post-transaction integration.	If financial buyers do not have functions already in place, they will need back-end infrastructure. Tend to scrutinize during due diligence and often seek to strengthen post-acquisition.

TAKE-AWAYS:

- The 5–20 Rule suggests that a potential acquirer for a business should be between five and twenty times the size of the business being acquired.
- Strategic buyers are companies that aim to acquire businesses whose products or services can be integrated into their existing operations to create long-term value.
- Financial buyers include private equity groups, acquisition entrepreneurs, family offices, and ESOPs. Related buyers include family, business partners, or management team members.
- Having clarity around your goals will enable you to pursue exit options that make the most sense for you. Because different types of buyers have fundamentally different goals, the way they approach your business in a M&A sale process can differ significantly.

--- MY ACTION PLAN ---

How can you use the 5–20 Rule to draw up a list of potential acquirers of your business?

Action Item	Resources Needed	Start By Date	Complete By Date

CHAPTER 7

YOU DON'T KNOW WHAT YOUR BUSINESS IS WORTH

It's far better to buy a wonderful company at a fair price, than a fair company at a wonderful price.

WARREN BUFFETT

You can't determine your company's value after hearing someone else's story. Paul Visokey, president of Stony Hill Advisors cautions, "Never trust somebody who sold their business, and told you they sold it for so much money that you can't believe it. Don't believe it."

As an owner, you know your business from the inside-out. The challenge (and opportunity) of strategic transition planning is to look at your business from the outside-in.

Why is this important?

Because we need to look at your company the way a potential buyer would.

That's why Chapter 6—focused on who should own your business after you—precedes this topic.

You need to put yourself in the buyer's shoes to look at your company as they would. What will your potential buyers look for?

If someone acquires your business, what is their future benefit? Potential buyers need a return on their investment . . . cash flows with risks they can manage effectively.

More predictable future cash flow means less risk and higher multiples.

Most of the companies in the US are privately held. According to the US Census Bureau, 60 percent of the US workforce is employed by a family-owned company. In 2022, the number of small businesses in the US reached 33.2 million, making up nearly all (99.9 percent) of US businesses.[31]

In the public company market, to see what a business is worth you can find it online in two seconds. The market cap is price per share times number of shares outstanding.

In the private company market, the valuation of a business has an infinite number of possible values. This is because private company valuations are determined ultimately by the buyer's perception of value and what deal terms are negotiated.

There are external and internal factors that impact business value.

External Factors

Generally speaking, external factors have an impact on your business and can be difficult to control or influence.

External Forces (No Control)		
Economy	Market Demand	Industry Forces
Barriers to Entry	Regulatory	Competition

A 2021 study by Pepperdine University spotlighted the leading external factors impacting value in privately held companies. The most dramatic result is that the most pressing problems facing private businesses currently are labor availability and the impact of COVID-19. The most troubling emerging issues are inflation and government regulation.[32]

- Impact from COVID-19 pandemic
- Government regulations and taxes
- Labor Availability
- Economic uncertainty (Domestic)
- Economic uncertainty (International)
- Political uncertainty
- Access to capital
- Competition from foreign trade partners
- Inflation

Internal Factors

Internal factors are value drivers that can be directly controlled and influenced by actions and decisions you make.

There is an inverse relationship between risk and value in your business. Ignoring important value drivers means you may have a less attractive, less transferable, less sellable . . . less valuable business.

Here are eight time-tested value drivers that we will explore more deeply in upcoming chapters:

The Eight Value Drivers

1. **Financial Performance**—historical revenue and profit performance, company size, industry, and quality of financial recordkeeping (covered in this chapter)
2. **Growth Potential**—ability to expand organically or via acquisitions (covered in this chapter and Chapter 11)
3. **Operational Risks**—addressable risks associated with key employees, customers, and suppliers (Chapter 9)
4. **Cash Flow**—ability to manage working capital requirements and service debt (Chapter 8)
5. **Recurring Revenue**—predictable stream of future cash flows from subscription or contracted agreements (Chapter 10)
6. **Competition**—what makes your business unique or differentiated in your industry (Chapter 11)
7. **Customer Satisfaction**—ability to attract, convert, and retain customers cost effectively (Chapter 10)
8. **Owner Involvement and Dependencies**—people, processes, and systems enabling the business to thrive without its owner (Chapter 3)

In this chapter, we'll dive into the first value driver, financial performance, and terminology related to business valuations as well as growth potential.

The first key performance indicator (KPI) to know for your business is revenue

Buyers will request to see your Profit and Loss (P&L) reports for the past three years. They may also want to see reports by month to determine TTM—trailing twelve-month revenue.

As an M&A intermediary, I have the benefit of experience communicating directly with buyers to understand what they are looking for. They are looking to identify potential risks in the cash flow of the business, and it all starts with top-line revenue.

Keep in mind that this book is intended to be a guide to your thinking. To guide our understanding of your company's potential, let's put ourselves in the mindset of the buyer.

Consider also that buyers looking for acquisitions have a series of analyses that they're doing to make sure the company is the right fit for them. Many companies are evaluating financials at a high level in the pre-LOI stage.

Revenue related questions buyers may have:

1. **Trending**—Are revenues going up or down? Has the revenue trajectory been flat? Are there explainable reasons for the trend you're experiencing? Would a new buyer be able to reverse that trend, and what investment would be required to do so?
2. **Outliers**—Were there any revenue outliers—any one-time clients or deals not expected to repeat?
3. **Resiliency**—How has the company performed during periods of economic crisis such as the COVID-19 pandemic in 2020? What were the company's top-line revenue trends one year prior to the crisis, and two years afterward? How was the company affected by market dynamics?

As a result of the COVID-19 pandemic, some businesses were bolstered while others struggled. One of my clients was deemed essential, and their business was not affected long term. I have another client who had a shutdown, but then was deemed essential and ramped back up quickly. I have another client who didn't miss a beat during the pandemic but is feeling the headwinds from recessionary factors.

If revenue trends are flat or declining, buyers may presume that there is more risk in the business. More risk means buyers apply more of a discount on the value of the business. A lower multiple means the buyer considers the business to have a higher risk profile. Generally speaking, businesses that are attractive to buyers, and that are readily transferable, will have higher valuations.

This is one reason why SaaS (software-as-a-service) or other recurring revenue businesses tend to have higher valuations. Because the predictability of future cash flows is higher with committed monthly subscribers or annual contracts.

Here are a few private company multiple definitions to be familiar with:

- EV—Enterprise Value
- EV/EBITDA—Most widely used. It is a proxy for pre-tax available cash flow to debt and equity. EBITDA stands for earnings before interest, taxes, and depreciation.
- EV/Sales—Typically used when the company has negative EBITDA or low margins.
- EV/SDE—Seller Discretionary Earnings is commonly used in the lower middle market for Adjusted Net Operating Income.

What's the difference between SDE and EBITDA?

EBITDA and SDE measure the performance of your business differently.

EBITDA allows investors to compare your business against others in the same industry by removing expenses that skew a fair comparison.

SDE tells an individual looking to acquire your business how much they would make if they worked full-time in the business. Seller's discretionary earnings adds back your full owner's salary and benefits to reflect what a full-time owner-operator would earn.

ADJUSTED EBITDA	SDE
The operating profit your business can provide to an investor after paying a fair manager's salary.	The total financial benefit your business can provide to one full-time owner-operator.

The Multiples Approach to Valuing

There are several ways to determine the value of a business. To keep it simple, let's consider the *multiples approach*, which follows two steps:

1. Take a simple measurement such as revenue or EBITDA (earnings before interest, tax, depreciation, and amortization).
2. Apply a multiplication factor based on industry sales or comparable companies in the sector.

While this approach may seem straightforward, there are many factors that need to be considered.

When I work on business valuations, I provide a fair and balanced outlook on the valuation of the business and share ways to improve its value before it is sold.

The fundamental rationale behind multiples-based valuation is that businesses in the same industry or sector should be valued based on their comparison to other similar businesses.

For example, a business with an EBITDA of $1 million, with comparable EBITDA multiples of between four and five times, would likely be valued between $4 million and $5 million.

SDE tells an individual looking to acquire your business how much they would make if they worked full-time in the business. The primary difference between SDE and EBITDA is in the adjustment for owner's salary. Adjusted EBITDA adds back any excessive owner's salary and benefits over what a manager would make.

The more organized your financials are, you'll be able to track which expenses or revenues to not include (or to include) as part of an add-back analysis.

SDE is calculated by taking your business's net profit and adding back or "recasting" certain discretionary expenses.

An "add-back" is an expense that is added back to find your SDE. Typical add-backs include your owner's salary, your payroll taxes on your salary, interest, depreciation, and any personal expenses paid through the business. Some add-backs are standard, they apply to every business. Other add-backs will depend on the specifics of your business.

Most businesses above $1 million in earnings will be valued with a multiple of EBITDA.

Private equity groups and strategic buyers will commonly value your company using a multiple of EBITDA.

Most businesses under $1 million in earnings will be valued using seller's discretionary earnings. Your business is most likely to sell to an individual buyer if it's in this size range. Individual buyers prefer to use SDE because it more accurately reflects the cash flow that will go in their pocket.

When it comes to discretionary expenses, it is important that you stay accountable to your numbers to know what's running through your business.

I did a business valuation for one of my clients and we took a deep dive into company expenses. There were discretionary expenses that I've commonly seen such as cell phones, car, and healthcare. Less typical expenses that we uncovered included $30,000 for snow removal and landscaping at his personal residence. Using a valuation multiplier of 3.5 times profit, meant an additional $100,000 of enterprise value. For a business valued around $1,000,000 it was a significant add-back.

Think of it this way. In the US, for every $1 in personal discretionary expenses you run through your company for toilet paper, you will save around 30 percent on taxes. Using the above example, you would save $0.30, but potentially lose $3.00 of value.

"You don't want to really give your future buyer a choice. You don't want to show up to your future buyer and say, "All these expenses here . . . well, you don't really need them to run the business. That's just my lifestyle. I have tickets to my favorite sports team or to the opera, or I like over-buying inventory because it just makes me feel better. It makes your company more profitable. Yes, you're going to be having higher taxes. But it's really a rounding error relative to the return on investment that you'll get from the liquidity event. What we like to suggest is if you can remove those add-backs and have a good two or three years. You're showing up to the future buyer saying, here it is no explanations. There's nothing to challenge. And you're better off for it.[33]

—*Jeffrey Feldberg, CEO, Deep Wealth Experience*

When we look at it that way, it's clear why good tracking is important. It's going to be a forcing mechanism to ask, "Why are we doing this?"

Kevin Urrutia and his brother founded Maid Sailors in New York City. They built up the business to 200 employees in four states before selling to a strategic buyer. "We had an idea of starting a business. In the beginning, we didn't plan it as well as we should have. All the finances were so intermingled and intertwined with personal stuff, business stuff, my other businesses. We were charging these credit cards like, 'Okay, this is going to fund our stock. This is going to fund my other company with this business's cash.' It was a complete mess. It took almost a year of stripping down all the numbers."[34]

As part of financial performance, two additional areas that influence value are Size and Industry.

Company Size

One of the primary factors driving value is the size of the business. Size does matter when we're talking about value.

Why is that? It's about the perception of risk. A company that is larger is perceived to be less risky because it is likely to be more well established and less reliant on the owner.

Said differently, there can be a small company discount. Companies that are under $1 million in revenue, referred to as Main Street businesses, tend to see lower multiples compared to similar companies in the same industry with $5 million in revenue or higher.

Larger companies also may have more access to capital, an important factor for growth. From the buyer perspective, a company with more predictable cash flow may be more able to service the debt from a lender—this is an especially important factor if you're planning to sell your business to an acquisition entrepreneur or someone seeking commercial financing.

There can be a perception from strategic and financial buyers that smaller companies are riskier. A buyer wants predictability of future cash flow. If your company is $1 million to $10 million in revenue, you may run into a "small company discount." How can you demonstrate that you're positioned for growth? Have you achieved product or service market fit? Do your profits show growth potential as well as your top-line revenues?

The relative power of buyers and sellers can be influenced by company size. In their research, Pepperdine asked business brokers whether they perceived a buyer's or seller's market during the prior year. Here's what they found:

	Deals valued under $499,999	Deals valued from $500,000 to $999,999	Deals valued from $1 million to $1.99 million	Deals valued from $2 million to $4.99 million	Deals valued from $5 million to $50 million
Buyer's market	80%	71%	54%	43%	37%
Seller's market	20%	29%	46%	57%	63%

The majority of business brokers perceived a "buyer's market" for deals valued under $2 million, with a flip to a "seller's market" for deals valued above $2 million.

Industry

Different industries are valued differently, and a big reason for that has to do with cash flows and working capital requirements. Looking at multiples of EBITDA, some industries tend to be weighted higher than others.

An industry that tends to float to the top is tech and software. A big reason why is because tech and software tend to have recurring revenue business models. I'll cover recurring revenue more deeply in another section.

Valuation ranges for $1 million to $3 million EBITDA companies[35]

FirstPageSage conducted an analysis of EBITDA multiples for small-to-midsized private businesses using data published in M&A and private equity publications. The table below provides a snapshot of private company valuations by industry for companies with $1 million to $3 million in EBITDA.

Sector	EBITDA Multiple Range
Construction	2.5x—7.4x
e-Commerce	5.4x—12.3x
Engineering	3.1x—7.3x
Environmental & Clean Energy	3.9x—11.6x
Financial Services	3.1x—6.6x
Healthcare	4.8x—8.1x
Industrial IoT	7.6x—17.2x
IT & Managed Services	4.5x—12.2x
Manufacturing	4.7x—9.3x
Oil & Gas	5.2x—8.1x
Staffing & Recruitment	4.7x—9.4x
Transportation & Logistics	5.1x—9.2x

The EBITDA multiples are averages. Achieving these multiples depends on the investor's weighting of value drivers as well as the business' strategic fit with the acquirer or portfolio.

Another important impact of financial performance is whether the business is "bankable."

If you have tried to get a commercial loan or Small Business Association (SBA) loan, you may have discovered that some banks prefer certain types of businesses versus other types of businesses.

What could make your business ineligible for a small business or commercial loan?

A bank manages exposure to certain risks and maintains institutional restrictions on industries or business models that are:

- Highly cyclical
- Dependent on discretionary spending
- Exhibit customer/revenue concentrations
- Do not have strong/reliable historic cash flow

I had a recent experience with two lenders, one is a national small business lender and the other is a regional bank providing conventional loans. Both banks shared their "Do Not Lend" industry list. Note that this is a consolidated list and varied between the two banks. Use this as a guide, rather than as an absolute, since different banks have different policies which vary from time to time.

The banks stated that they are looking for businesses with established cash flow and recurring revenue streams.

- Gas stations
- Convenience stores
- Liquor stores
- Golf courses
- Car washes—limited to auto vertical on a case-by-case basis
- Spas/massage parlors

- Residential construction / general contractors / businesses tied to new construction
- E-commerce where there is reliance on a concentrated distribution channel such as Amazon or emphasis on the sale of a single generic commodity
- Independent restaurants
- Delivery route drivers
- Trucking
- Boat dealers
- Online trading academies
- Landscaping/lawn services—company should have barriers to entry, contract revenue, low seasonality and not tied to new construction
- Mortgage companies (extreme cyclicality)
- Art galleries (inconsistent earnings)
- Non-doctor owned medical practices
- Co-working franchises
- Sports complexes
- Pet store franchises
- Family entertainment and hospitality businesses—evaluate if severe covid impacts and ongoing industry concerns
- Emergency rooms

There are various reasons why your company's multiple might be at the higher—or lower—range of value.

As part of strategic transition planning, I provide clients with a valuation analysis to understand your industry multiples and identify ways to make your company more valuable compared to your competition.

A company that has strong growth potential and ability to scale is more likely to get premium offer. The key question is whether your business can handle a 5x increase in demand?

If you answered "no," you're not alone. Many businesses struggle with the notion of scale.

- How much additional staff would need to be added?
- What would your operating expenses look like?
- Would you need to add equipment, infrastructure, or capital expenses to handle the growth?
- Will you fund the growth through operating cash flow or business loans?
- What is cost or risk to achieve the growth?

For each customer that you add, do your profits go up, down, or stay flat?

If your company generates $1000 in profit from 100 customers annually, your profit per customer is $10. If your company served 200 customers, what would your profit per customer be?

Another way to evaluate growth potential is looking at the subsets of a market.

- TAM or Total Available Market is the total market demand for a product or service.
- SAM or Serviceable Available Market is the segment of the TAM targeted by your products and services which is within your geographical reach.
- SOM or Serviceable Obtainable Market is the portion of SAM that you can capture.

Let's say you are selling butter. Your TAM would be the worldwide butter market. If you were present in every country and had no competition you would generate TAM as revenues.

Not very realistic. Let's say you are starting your butter brand in two cities where the demand for butter can be estimated based on: population, food habits, and revenues generated by grocery stores and restaurants in other cities having similar demographics. This is your Serviceable Available Market: the demand for your type of products within your reach market.

Likely you are not the only butter supplier in these cities. You can capture a fraction of your serviceable market. Most likely you can attract butter fanatics in restaurants and a fraction of the people located further away that are willing to give your butter a try for the sake of fast-food diversity. This is your Serviceable Obtainable Market (SOM).

Put yourself in a buyer's shoes. Buyers may be looking to invest in opportunities which offer substantial upside potential and de-risk the investment.

The SOM and SAM help de-risk the investment while the TAM assesses upside potential.

The Serviceable Obtainable Market is your company's short-term target and the one that matters the most.

If you are not able to demonstrate success in a local market, chances are that your company will not succeed at capturing a larger market—regional, national, or international.

Your SOM includes:

- Your product: people will want to buy what you produce
- Your marketing plan and the identified distribution channels: you have a clear plan to reach a large portion of your target customers
- Your SAM and the strength of your competition

For the buyer, the ability to reach your SOM means that they will not lose their shirt. SAM acts as a good proxy for the short-term upside potential of your business.

If you can deliver SOM then you are capable and credible, and you might be able to increase the market share and reach a more important penetration of the SAM which would deliver a good return on investment.

Under Canvas, the glamping company co-founded by Sarah Dusek and her husband, reached a position of market leadership by capitalizing on their Serviceable Obtainable Market. They were focused on their customer demographic, developed a marketing plan, and identified cost efficient channels to reach a large portion of their target customers.

"Finding Purpose After Selling The Business"
Sarah Dusek, Co-Founder, Under Canvas and
General Partner, Enygma Ventures
Succession Stories Podcast E94[36]

"I talk about this all the time because I now invest in small businesses. One of the things we are constantly looking for is how to find your highly scalable growth channel that is relatively low cost. You're always looking for a route to market that isn't going to cost the earth. Part of our strategy was to go where the people were. We discovered that there was an overabundance of people traveling to national parks and an under supply of accommodations to stay in.

Our highly scalable growth channel was moving into markets where there just wasn't enough accommodation, and leveraging what was already in that space, TripAdvisor, Expedia, booking.com, to enable us to acquire customers. We leveraged what existed and plugged holes where no one existed. It was like trying to discover where's the hole that I can fit in. How can I use what's already out there to push people toward me because I had virtually no money. We were trying to find ways to market ourselves. This was before Facebook, so Facebook marketing wasn't really a thing. It was trying to find ways to be in front of our target audience. That's what I tell people all the time, how can you go where your audience already is? How can you show up in front of them in the most efficient, most cost-effective way to get your products or services seen.

If we did a good job, and this is true for most companies, if your guest or your customer has a great experience with you, and they fall in love with you, they're going to be your best advocate for your product or service. They're going to tell their friends and family about you. We had some curb appeal and that definitely helped and people did love our experience. Even our very early, minimal viable product experience people loved and raved about. That was huge for us getting great organic traffic."

Another example of a company driving value through its growth potential is AfterMail. John Warrillow interviewed the founder of After-Mail on his podcast, *Built to Sell*.

Rod Drury founded AfterMail in 2004. The software product that he developed provided a better way to archive old emails. Soon after Sarbanes-Oxley became a federal law in the U.S., companies were required to have a method for storing their emails. Drury's AfterMail allowed companies to store their emails in a more effective, efficient manner. He convinced two charter companies, both were Fortune 500 companies, to purchase and use AfterMail. Each contract for the software was around a million dollars each, which gave AfterMail a revenue of $2 million.

Put yourself in Rod's shoes. With two Fortune 500 customers in hand, do you go out and hire a team of salespeople to call on the other 498 Fortune 500 companies? Or do you do what Rod did? Which was something different.

Rod recognized that he could demonstrate to an acquirer that there was significant future potential in his business and convince them that there was ample field left to plow.

Rod convinced Quest Software, who had all the Fortune 500 as clients, to spend $35 million to buy his $2 million software company.

Notably, $15 million of the $35 million was paid in cash up front.

What was Quest's rationale into the acquisition? Quest recognized the value of AfterMail because they have the other 498 companies that need this software. With the new legislation, speed was of the essence. The clients needed the software immediately based on the new legislation. It would have taken Quest years to develop something that AfterMail had already created.

For that growth potential, Quest was willing to spend an enormous amount of money to buy his business.

Had Rod gone out and ploddingly over a twenty- or thirty-year period built and sold to the other 498 companies, Quest could have built a competitive product and taken away market share from AfterMail to undermine the value of their company. But Rod Drury had the discipline to sell when there was still lots of field left to plow in his business.

Growth potential encompasses your growth trajectory combined with the vision the buyer has for your business.

I offer a business readiness assessment where one of the questions is, "What is your biggest fear when it comes to selling your business?"

The most common answer I've seen across hundreds of responses from small business owners is: "Not getting the value I think my business is worth."

A company that is profitable year over year, but isn't growing, will face a caution sign. If you're not growing your business, you're exiting. You may be headed toward Death Valley and will be out of business at some point. Value buyers will look at your business as a turnaround opportunity and offer a low-ball price.

If you're keeping a scorecard for your business (and I hope you are) this is an important metric to track. It's critical to know this information when time is on your side to make changes. Otherwise you may be disappointed when offers are lower than you expect. Don't wait until it's too late.

"The less time and effort you'll put into the process, or the worse shape you're in the beginning, the longer it takes to be ready. The one thing I will assure you is if you're not ready, that will be brought to the light of day in the buy side due diligence by any reasonably capable suitor."
—*Jeffrey Ford, Founding Partner, Grossman Yanak and Ford*
Succession Stories Podcast E86[37]

TAKE-AWAYS

- In the private markets, company value is determined by the buyer. You can't look up the value on Yahoo! Finance and see what the price is like you can for a public company.

- Look at your company through the lens of a buyer to understand potential value and risk.

- Have a consistent method of accurately tracking the financials of your business.

- Track your personal expenses and other add-backs in the business to maximize profitability.

- Multiples-based valuation methods involve comparing a business to others in the same industry or sector to determine its value.

- Several value drivers (external and internal) can impact the valuation multiple applied to your business. Different buyers reward different value drivers differently.

MY ACTION PLAN

How can you discover what your business is worth and what impacts the value of your business?

Action Item	Resources Needed	Start By Date	Complete By Date

CHAPTER 8

YOU NEED TO IMPROVE CASH FLOW

The road to success is always under construction.

LILY TOMLIN

Businesses are valued based on their ability to generate cash flows, and a business is sold based on the expectation that it will generate future profits. The more cash flow a business can generate and secure, the more it will be worth.

Industry cyclicality can impact whether your company generates predictable cash flows. Seasonal businesses or industries with demand fluctuations based on prevailing economic conditions can impact the attractiveness and risk of the business. Lines of credit may be required to fuel working capital during slower periods.

What Is Cash Flow?

Cash flow is the net amount of cash going in and out of a business. A company's success is determined by its ability to create positive cash flows through the normal course of its business operations. Cash coming into a company, or inflows, are revenues from the sale of goods or services as well as income from investments. Cash going out of a company, or outflows, are expenses and debt payments.

What Is Working Capital?

As discussed previously, in most M&A transactions, the buyer and seller arrive at a purchase price by multiplying the target company's earnings before interest, taxes, depreciation, and amortization (EBITDA) by an agreed-upon multiple.

The other part of the equation for purchase price is working capital. Working capital is a critical component in the operation of a business. It can be a signal of the company's health and a significant factor in determining a company's value.

Working capital is calculated by subtracting current liabilities from current assets. A company's level of working capital impacts value because changes in working capital impacts cash flow and valuation is inherently tied to cash flow.

For example, if a company has $100,000 in current assets and $40,000 in current liabilities the working capital of the business is $60,000.

Working capital can also be presented as a ratio. Current assets divided by current liabilities. In the above example, the working capital ratio would be 2.5.

Working capital ratios represent how many times the company can pay off its current liabilities using its current assets. It is a measure of the short-term financial well-being of the business. A company with a low ratio (close to one or less) may be experiencing financial difficulties. A general rule, for most non-seasonal industries, is that a company should be able to fund three 3 months of its expenses using its current assets.

If a company holds "excess working capital," the excess amount is considered additional value and is classified as a non-operating asset.

Across different companies, working capital requirements can be different even for businesses in the same industry. For example, a landscaping business in New Jersey will have more seasonality in revenue than a landscaping firm in Florida.

In a mature company with relatively stable operations, working capital is often calculated by taking an average of the most recent twelve-month period.

In a rapidly growing company, receivables and inventories may be increasing monthly, requiring higher working capital. In these types of situations, it may be more realistic to calculate working capital based using an average over the last three months.

If a company typically receives payment before a product or service is delivered, the company may operate with negative working capital. This means that the liabilities that need to be paid within one year exceed the current assets that are monetizable over the same period.

One example of a company with negative working capital is Dell Computers. Michael Dell focused the company on the cash conversion cycle, which consists of inventory, payables, receivables, and cash flow from operations. Dell sold direct to customers and carried little finished-goods inventory. The company bought components on a just-in-time basis and low parts inventory. Because customers often paid Dell more quickly than the company paid suppliers, cash flow was positive and working capital was negative.[38]

If this is your business model, you might expect to have discussions during negotiations about some or all the cash being left in the business at the time of the sale.

Another aspect to working capital is whether it is more predictable or erratic. Working capital can become erratic when customers change payment habits or terms, customer payments are large and infrequent, companies acquire inventory in large lots, or there are changes in payment patterns to vendors.

When evaluating your business, here are some aspects to consider:

- What is normal working capital for the industry?
- What is working capital as a percentage of sales?
- What special circumstances cause the company's working capital to vary from normal levels?
- How significantly does inventory vary on a month-to-month basis?
- How is working capital affected by seasonal sales?
- Are the business and its working capital needs growing?

Inflationary pressures can also impact cash flow and working capital, and ultimately, the value of your business. If inflation is impacting the profitability of your company, and the business is unable to pass increased costs to customers, your business will be worth less.

For a business to maintain or increase its value, it must be growing. Companies that are more sensitive to inflation are valued lower than businesses that can maintain their profits by passing cost increases on to customers. A devastating effect of inflation is lower customer demand for discretionary goods and services, leading to lower profits.

In times of inflation, companies may see a rise in overhead expenses, such as long-term lease agreements that contain escalation clauses tied to inflationary measures. Higher wage demand can create pressures to retain skilled labor in a tighter labor market. Vendors and professional service providers to your business may also increase their prices during times of inflation.

Does your business have deficient working capital levels?

1. Yes, if your company has ongoing difficulty meeting its current liability obligations using its current assets.
2. Yes, if your company has a positive working capital balance, but is insufficient to support growth initiatives and runs as status quo.

Some of the items that should be considered in the determination of a working capital surplus or deficiency include:

- Comparison to industry norms for top performing companies
- Revenue to working capital ratios
- Seasonality
- Growth capital expenditure requirements
- Inventory turns
- Accounts receivable days
- Accounts payable days
- Maximum amount of operating line of credit or cash available
- If surplus working capital is being used to gain purchasing discounts

How Can You Increase Cash Flow?

Ways to increase cash flow for a business include offering discounts for early payments, leasing not buying, improving inventory, conducting consumer credit checks, and using high-interest savings accounts.

One of my clients owns seven-figure revenue marketing agency. I encouraged him to make small changes to improve cash flow by taking a fresh look at his payment policies.

"When do you invoice clients?" I asked. He said, "We bill when services are delivered and invoice with net thirty terms." This meant many client payments were received sixty days or more from when services were rendered.

I asked cheekily, "What if you change that policy?"

"There's no reason we can't," the owner said. "I just hadn't thought about it before."

For all new clients, new contract terms were implemented immediately. They asked for an upfront deposit and thirty-day billing cycle instead of when services delivered. These changes enabled the company to create a subscription model rather than operate as a project-based model.

One of the other tools at the disposal of a small business owner is to think about your payment terms as vendor financing. Are invoices due upon receipt or do you have terms: net thirty, sixty, or ninety days? If your company has net thirty now, what if you asked for net ninety? Increasing payment terms is like getting vendor financing to help improve your operating cash flow.

Here's an assignment. Take a fresh look at your cash flow and working capital requirements with these two questions in mind:

1. What are ideas for getting customers' receivables sooner (Money In)?
2. What are ideas for slowing down payables to vendors (Money Out)?

Let's examine your working capital and cash flow from operations:

- Are you borrowing to satisfy the needs of your business to pay employees, rent, supplies?
- Is there a seasonality to your business that makes cash flow "lumpy" certain times of the year?
- What are your policies with invoicing?
- What are your policies for accounts payable? Who's responsible in your company for accounts receivable? Do you have a buttoned-up process for that?

In my business owner and CEO workshops, this topic usually stimulates a lot of discussion. Some people have raised concerns, "I really pride myself on paying my vendors quickly because I'm a small business too." I hear you on that, we're not trying to put your vendors out of business.

Here are ideas from other entrepreneurs. Perhaps these will help you develop some of your own:

How Can You Get Customers' Money Sooner?

- "Bill more frequently. We only bill once a week now, so making that twice a week and then increasing our admin staff in our billing department so they can do more follow ups on outstanding bills."
- "We only accept bank transfers and credit card payments. At the time we sign a contract, we also get pre-approval for autopay. So we charge like rent. We charge at the beginning of the service and that covers the next thirty days. But it's always with pre-approval. So we're not waiting for the client. They've signed an agreement allowing us to withdraw that money, either electronic funds transfer or credit card."
- "Relook at the payment schedule for upfront and final deposits. We take the final payment from individual homeowners the day

we do the installation and negotiate the rest. Having someone besides me do the negotiations, like my general manager, and start to have those conversations."

- "We started taking credit card authorization forms for medium sized projects where we're dealing directly with the consumer. We're doing multiple payments rather than waiting till the very end to try to get our final 50 percent. I set up a payment schedule such that we're maybe only owed 10 percent or 20 percent at the end of the project so that we get more of our money up front or throughout the process."

- "We work with a lot of startup companies, and hold the bag at the end of the project when it either doesn't get off the ground or they lose funding. We have talked about having an escrow account that is equal to the retainer that is to be untouched until the end of the project. At which point it would either be applied to the last payment that we don't ever seem to get or be refunded to the customer."

- "Most of my customers are credit card currently. For larger orders, we could require a 30 percent or 50 percent deposit. We do that for custom orders already, but this would be for larger orders and that would save on credit card fees. We talked about potentially switching to Venmo or Zelle accepting those payments to speed up getting the money."

How Can You Slow Down Payments to Vendors?

- "We have a mandatory thirty-day net to make payments, and that includes contractors who decide to work with us. Creative agencies often subcontract creative work. Whenever possible, we pay with a credit card. Then that payment isn't due for another thirty days. That gives us about sixty days window where we're controlling our cash. We don't run balances on the credit cards, we pay them off, but we use them as a tool to give us an extra thirty days."

- "I'm on fifteen day payable terms with one of my vendors. Five years ago, I got behind and I pay them weekly. I would like to negotiate with them to get it back to thirty days. I would like to hang on to the cash a little bit longer."

- "We pay our contractors on the same schedule as we pay our employees because we treat them kind of like employees. I don't really want to change that, but I was thinking it might be interesting to offer them to accept their payment via credit card instead of direct deposit. That way in lieu of a net thirty, they could have a choice. You can either get paid net thirty via direct deposit or you can get the money right away if you'll accept a credit card. That would give us thirty days to pay it off. That could help us in the long run, and it would help us build our travel points. We charge a convenience fee to offset that and then the points add up."

- "For monthly commissions paid to my sales reps, we pay a fee for wire transfers. I've switched a lot of them to Zelle or Venmo to reduce the fees. It's not necessarily slowing it down, but at least reducing some of the additional fees and expenses and paying out large sums. I feel like there's more there with Venmo and Zelle that I do need to look more into."

Exercise: Which cash flow ideas may be a fit for your business?

Accelerate Cash "In"	Delay Cash "Out"
Increase deposits	Vendor financing—inventory terms
Push industry standards—create rules to adhere: payment terms, "start date," "invoice date"	Vendor managed inventory
Late payment fees	Lease don't buy
Offer discounts for early payment	Credit card with suppliers

Factoring receivables	Inventory consignment—take in materials and pay when used
Retainer revenue model	Hedging
More aggressive accounts receivable process—people and technology	Form a buying cooperative
Credit card fees factored into contract price	Time temporary labor payment at end of month with credit card
Program selling—get clients on a schedule	Negotiate payment terms contractually
Conduct customer credit checks—credit scoring if offer terms, or use to disqualify customers	
Use electronic payments	
Credit collection management—quicker action with delinquent accounts and collection services	
Buy-in membership model, get upfront payments	
Charge for services like scoping and go/no-go decisions to fund projects	
100 percent upfront payment on custom product orders	
Develop relationship with vendor's AP department	
Set up lockbox service with bank to expedite the collection of paper-based payments and provide timely payment information to update accounts receivable records	

Milestone billing versus progress billing- Milestone may bring in cash sooner. Once specific deliverables are reached, the customer pay an agreed amount. Progress payments only allow for regular percentage payments of the entire contract.	
Implement a blanket purchase order with customer up to certain a dollar amount	
Annualized fee—steady cash flow	

Recall the earlier discussion about financial buyers. These can be private equity groups, acquisition entrepreneurs, or family offices where the buyer is looking for the best deal to acquire an ongoing company. Unlike strategic acquirers, there are likely no other synergies to offset expenses.

This is especially important when a buyer is intending to live off the income from the ongoing business. The buyer must be able to repay whatever the source of funding is for the business, whether it's a bank loan or personal funds. They need to make sure that the cash flow supports the return on investment.

TAKE-AWAYS:

- Healthy cash flow is the result of operations that run efficiently and smoothly. Understand ways to reduce cash flow risk in your business.
- When it comes to payables, look to reducing expenses as well as timing of payments.
- Implementing some or all the ideas in this section should help you increase your business's cash flow. You'll also want to consider implications of changes to your policies on customer service, product development, and marketing.
- Having strong cash flow enables your business to be bankable to potential buyers, a critical consideration if they are seeking a conventional bank loan or an SBA loan.

MY ACTION PLAN

What are some specific ways you plan to improve the cash flow of your business?

Action Item	Resources Needed	Start By Date	Complete By Date

RISK TRIPWIRES CAN HURT TRANSFERABILITY

Curious things, habits. People themselves
never knew they had them.

AGATHA CHRISTIE

I chose this quote from Agatha Christie not because business transition planning is a mystery, although you might say that it is even at Chapter 9.

To me it conjures an image of not seeing things right in front of us. Which is why if you don't look for the risk tripwires in your company, you may find them when it's too late to do anything about them.

I encourage my clients to take a strategic inventory to understand their important assets. Understanding the types of assets (tangible and intangible) and their relative transferability can drive value in the business and influence the type of transaction structure you should look for if you intend to sell to a third-party.

If you took an inventory of all the assets in your business, what would you put on your list?

You may have tangible assets including:

- Furniture, fixture, and equipment (FFE)
- Vehicles—leased and owned
- Inventory
- Owner insurance policies (e.g. life, disability)

And, you may have intangible assets including:

- Intellectual property—patents, trademarks
- Customer database
- Brand identity & reputation
- Industry knowledge
- Process documentation

- Industry licenses and certifications
- Vendor agreements
- Lease agreements
- Customer contracts
- Websites
- Domain names
- Small business owner designations (e.g. woman, veteran, minority, etc.)

Now consider how difficult it would be to transfer these assets to a new owner. Assign each asset a transferability score on a range of 1= highly difficult, 5 = easy.

Asset List	Transferability Score	Ideas to Improve Transferability

Small Business Owner Designations

There are various federal, local government and private sector diversity certifications available to business owners that can help open doors to public and private sector revenue sources.

The US Small Business Administration offers certification programs like the Woman-Owned Business Enterprise (WBE), Minority Business Enterprise (MBE), Veteran Owned Business, HUBZone Program, 8(a) Business Development Program, and Lesbian, Gay, Bisexual, Transgender, Queer (LBGTQ) Owned Business Enterprise which make businesses eligible for certain government contracts and provide access to resources.[39]

To qualify, your business must be owned, operated, managed, and controlled by a person or persons who identify for the designation. This means that at the business must be at least 51 percent owned by one or more people with the designation who work daily within the business full-time.

After you've been certified, you will need to apply for recertification on an ongoing basis typically every two to five years, depending on the specific certification or issuing entity. This means you will need to maintain and prove certain eligibility standards throughout each recertification interval.

There are various scenarios that could affect a change in your ownership and status of your certifications:

- Recapitalization—take on additional investors, affecting your ownership percentage
- Retirement—when you no longer work in your company full-time
- Sale—sell the business outright to a third-party
- Acquisition—purchase an existing WBE, MBE, or veteran firm

If your business has one or more of these certifications, you'll need to consider how important they are to the success of your business when considering a change in ownership.

Consider whether the certifications must transfer to a new owner for the business to thrive. This can influence your thinking about who will own your business after you. Develop criteria for who would be an ideal buyer of your business.

Obtaining these certifications can be time consuming, and you may not want to compromise them. Prepare for changes in ownership well in advance. Work with legal advisors who are knowledgeable in this area as it could mean the difference between continued certification or de-certification.

When it comes to evaluating risks in your business, there can be many blind spots. Finding those tripwires before it's too late is important. In this chapter, I spotlight three additional areas of focus: customers, suppliers, and key employees.

Customer Risk

Does your business have significant customer concentration? As a general rule, no single customer should account for more than 15 percent of total revenue.

Losing a key customer due to unforeseen circumstances, or a declined contract renewal, can present significant risks to your business.

Answer these questions to understand potential risks you may be facing:

- What percent of total revenue comes from your largest customers?
- What would happen to your company if these customers decided to take their business elsewhere?
  - My company would thrive
  - My company would suffer, but recover
  - My company would face significant issues and may not recover

- What percent of total revenue comes from a single industry? Again, your business may face significant revenue risks if your target industry heads into an economic downturn.

How could you mitigate these risks?

Having contracts can be an answer but not all contracts are created equally. Many privately held companies have "hand-shake deals" with customers who have been doing business with them for years and years.

I faced this issue at a prior company. There was no paper contract between the companies because the top executive had a made an informal agreement. The agreement lasted for twenty years until the executives retired. Then our client put our business up for bid, and the top-to-top relationship transitioned to a procurement department negotiation.

Remember—risks related to concentration and revenue transferability can have an impact on your valuation multiple.

Customer Satisfaction, Acquisition, and Churn

"Your most unhappy customers are your greatest sources of learning."
—*Bill Gates*

As entrepreneurs, you're in the business of solving problems for customers in exchange for value. It's good to know if customers are not happy with your business. It's also good to understand what your customers' pain points are because maybe you'll find a better solution than your competitors.

Customer satisfaction is an important measure. Having a quantifiable measurement gives a sense of how happy your customers are and how long they purchase from you. Long-term relationships are key to your business's success. It's crucial to maintain strong relationships with your past and existing clients, so they stay loyal.

High rates of customer churn are generally perceived as a negative because it creates the need for new customer acquisition efforts.

Having a high customer retention rate is in your company's best interest. It generally costs five times as much to attract a new customer than to keep an existing one. Increasing customer retention by 5 percent can increase profits from 25–95 percent.

If you have difficult customers that aren't profitable to serve, you might be happy about them moving on. Generally, the more customer "churn" you have in your business, the more costly it will be to replace new customers by acquiring new ones.

How Do You Calculate Customer Acquisition Costs (CAC)?

CAC = Total marketing and sales costs for customer acquisition / Total number of customers acquired

Sales and marketing costs include:

- commissions paid to your sales team
- expenses for marketing, advertising, trade shows, digital marketing
- travel expenses when calling on prospects
- cost of conducting customer surveys
- and more

For example, if your business spends $100,000 per year to support your sales efforts and $50,000 on marketing, and you gain 100 new clients per year, your CAC is $1,500 = ($100,000 + $50,000)/100.

In addition to CAC, it's important to measure churn rates.

Customer churn rate shows how well (or poorly) your company is doing at retaining customers. The customer churn rate is calculated for a specific period of time—one month is reasonable for many businesses and allows you to spot trends in time to fix problems before they become disasters. You do not want to let an entire year go by without measuring customer churn.

Customer Churn = Number of customers lost that month / Number of customers at the start of the month

For example, if you start the month with fifty customers and lose five during the month, your customer churn rate is 10 percent (note that customer retention = 1 minus customer churn percentage, so the retention rate in this example is 90 percent). Keep in mind the time-period you use to calculate churn.

While 10 percent may not sound terrible, if you lose 10 percent of your customers per month, after a year, only about 28 percent of your original customers will still be with you.

You can often learn more from customers who leave, than from the ones you retain. Be sure to analyze the reasons why you lost customers. Maybe you'll discover pricing, operational, or service issues.

Revenue churn rate is important in evaluating the impact of customer churn for companies with recurring revenue. Recurring revenue is critical to business stability.

Amount of recurring revenue lost that month / Original amount of revenue for the month

For example, if your company has $500,000 in recurring revenue at the beginning of the month and loses customers representing $50,000 of that total, the revenue churn rate for the month is 10 percent.

Additionally, we need to understand the importance of bringing in new customers, but do you know the actual cost of acquiring those customers and the actual value to your business they represent?

The concepts of Customer Acquisition Cost, or CAC, and its close cousin, Customer Lifetime Value (CLTV), are critical to understanding whether the money you spend to attract new customers is ultimately a good investment for your business.

What's the rate at which these customers are leaving you? And if we have higher customer satisfaction scores, it should correlate nicely with lower customer acquisition costs and lower churn numbers.

"Scaling and Selling a Services Business"
Kevin Urrutia, Co-Founder, Maid Sailors
Succession Stories Podcast E54[40]

Kevin Urrutia's NYC cleaning company, Maid Sailors, was an "Uber for maid services." To scale, they provided quality service and implemented an online strategy focused on generating customer ratings and reviews.

Laurie Barkman:
What do you think made your company attractive to buyers?

Kevin Urrutia:
Number one, people were looking at us saying, "How are you guys growing so fast compared to other companies in the space?" Our rankings on Google were really high so we had really good SEO (Search Engine Optimization) rankings. If you searched for maid service NYC, home cleaning NYC, we were number one or two. That was a key thing for us.

Another thing for any cleaning company or service-based business is reviews. Having great reviews on Google Plus (back then), Google Maps now, or Yelp as well. Especially if you're in New York City, Yelp is big. People were asking, "How are you guys getting so many reviews?" For service companies, those are the things you look at, because no one wants to acquire a company that's two stars.

A review tells you everything about how the company is run. If you get a 4.55 star, that means something's happening. Then people are like, "These guys are running it well." A 2-star you automatically think, "These guys have no clue how to run the company, or at least they're not addressing any issues if it's consistently two stars." For us, that's a key indicator. When we're looking to acquire a company, we want 4+ stars because that means something's working. Anything below, the founder-owner doesn't care. That's the way we think about it."

Key Employee Risk

A key employee is usually the owner, founders, or a small number of employees. The main qualifying point is whether the person's absence would cause major financial harm to the company.

Attributes of key employees include:

- Subject matter expertise
- Industry knowledge
- Rainmaker drives significant revenue
- Relationships with customers or vendors
- Involvement with critical projects or processes
- Senior executives with experience, organizational knowledge, and relationships
- Other employees who are critical for a successful transition to new ownership

"Succession of Culture After Tragedy Strikes" Jennifer Ake Marriott, President, AKE Environmental Succession Stories Podcast E99[41]

Jennifer Ake Marriott is the second-generation President of AKE Environmental. She recounted what it was like after her aunt, a key employee at the family business, unexpectedly passed away.

Jennifer Ake Marriott:
The first problem was payroll. That was the immediate thing, we had to get checks out to people. I had some bookkeeping experience so I could figure out some of that stuff. It was a research project in so many ways. Everything that was on her desk, I studied every Post-It and her desk pad. I kept everything for at least two years. Every piece of mail that came in. I didn't have a context for a lot of things. I didn't know how important one thing was compared to another.

It's one of the issues that happens in a closely held family business. There aren't committed written processes or documentation for some of the activity that goes on, because you're talking about it all the time. You see these people all the time. It doesn't feel necessary, it feels redundant, and you don't have time for that anyway, because you're wearing five other hats.

Coming in on the backside of that, and not having a roadmap for anything, it was a real learning process. Then trying to interpret what she was doing within something. It's challenging. We got through it. Allow yourself a little grace. You don't know everything. Balls will be dropped. You just hope that they're not the big ones.

Laurie Barkman:
What should a business owner do to de-risk the business, given your experience?

Jennifer Ake Marriott:
One thing that would have helped would have been a one-page strategic plan. It would have helped me understand what I was stepping into. In a small business, especially a family or closely held business, you're talking all the time. It seems like a redundant task. Even if it doesn't totally get followed, it gives someone the idea of what I'm thinking about or striving for. If I could have understood the weaknesses, or the threats, that my aunt after twenty years in the business perceived, it would have saved me a ton of time not have to discover that on my own.

The second thing is start having that conversation. If something were to happen to you, the owner, that should obviously already be spelled out somewhere in your corporate documents. Who are the key people in your company that you need right now, and you're going to need on the backside? Bringing those people in, having those conversations once a year even to say, "By the way, if something were to happen to me, this is what's going to happen." Something happening might not be that you die, you could be just incapacitated. Have a plan and lay it out for people.

The last thing is that a lot of small businesses have what I used to refer to as the oral tradition. Everything is spoken, nothing is documented. Do as much documentation as possible. For accounting, make monthly notes for big purchases or anything out of the norm. Leave breadcrumbs. Tell the story so that if somebody walks in, they know what was happening. Those things are important in the face of disaster that you can do right now."

For continuity of operations, key person insurance offers a financial cushion if the sudden loss of a certain individual would profoundly negatively affect the company's operations. The death benefit gives the company time to find a new person or to implement other strategies to save (or shut down) the business.

The benefit can be used to cover the costs of recruiting, hiring, and training a replacement for the deceased person. If the company doesn't believe it can continue operations, it can use the money to pay off debts, distribute money to investors, provide severance benefits to employees, and shut down the business in an orderly manner. Key person insurance gives the company more options other than immediate bankruptcy.

Your ability to attract, retain, and develop key employees can enhance the transferability of your company. If you are considering a sale to a third-party, potential buyers will want to understand your assessment. Questions buyers may ask include:

- Who are your top sales representatives?
- Who would do the most damage if they went to the competition?
- Who is critical for product or service delivery?
- Who shoulders most of the workload in the company?
- Who has participated in critical business projects?
- Who has the customer relationships?
- What are the intentions of key management or employees to work in the business (are they planning to retire?)

Key employees are essential to business continuity after the sale. Deciding when and how to involve key employees is important because their retention may affect the selling price or kill the deal altogether. The buyer may make the offer contingent upon the key employees staying on after the deal closes.

A business owner who is worried about confidentiality may decide not to tell key employees ahead of time about their intention to sell. By not involving key employees in the sale process, some people may feel disrespected and decide to leave. Even worse would be taking other employees with them.

If key employees leave during due diligence, it could derail the sales process and paralyze business operations. If key employees leave after the sale is completed, and you have an earnout, it could cost you.

If a key employee leaves, business owners can prevent them from soliciting other employees for recruitment purposes by using non-solicitation agreements.

Non-compete agreements may prohibit the employee from leaving for a competitor or starting a competing business when selling your business. However, proposed changes by the Federal Trade Commission could radically change restrictive covenants law in the US. Companies may want to evaluate the business justification and scope of non-compete clauses for employment agreements and M&A activity.

There are different incentives you can use to drive retention amongst your key employees.

Higher Salaries

Key employees need to be well compensated before and during the transfer of your business. Higher salaries limit the chances of disruption while giving the new owner more reasons to trust that key employees will continue to perform even after the business changes hands.

Stay Bonus

A stay bonus provides a financial incentive to stay through the sales process and for a period after closing. Employees get a percentage of the bonus at closing, another percentage after 12 months, etc. to assist with transition and integration. Stay bonuses are usually offered to critical roles in finance such as a CFO or Controller.

Phantom Stock[42]

A phantom stock plan is a benefit that gives key employees advantages of owning stock in the company without giving them any company stock. Phantom stock agreements may be contingent upon a business sale, with the amount based on a percentage of the transaction value. A key employee may have a "phantom equity" deal to receive 0.5 percent of the sale proceeds. This provides a reason to perform through the transaction and stay on after the sale.

It is beneficial for all parties involved in the deal for the management team to have "skin in the game" and closely aligned incentives.

In some cases, the existing management team may roll over some or all of its equity into the newly acquired company and may even contribute additional capital alongside the financial sponsor.

Rollover equity is an additional source of funds, reducing the amount of leverage necessary and the equity contribution from the financial sponsor to complete the deal.

If a management team is willing to roll over some equity into the new entity, it implies confidence in the deal; the risk they are taking is worth the potential upside.

Supplier Risk

While some degree of risk has always been inherent in vendor relationships, some suppliers present more risk than others.

Supplier risks are situations or events affecting companies that provide goods or services to your business, potentially causing financial, operational, or reputational damage. During the COVID-19 pandemic, supply chains were challenged, and companies faced new levels of risk in these areas.

Some suppliers present more risk than others, depending on a variety of factors including how essential they are to your business, how much they can burn you if something does go wrong, and how easily they can be replaced by another supplier. The key is identifying and mitigating vendor risk before threats turn into crises.

Some supplier risk is greater than others. If your landscaper quits, you will have to contend with uncut grass until you find someone else. You have a much bigger problem if the vendor who maintains your network goes out of business the same day your systems crash.

Companies you do business with face financial risks of their own which can impact your organization. Financial challenges in these areas can distract a supplier from fulfilling its obligations to your organization, degrade the quality of its services, or even cause it to cease operations altogether—causing a break in your supply chain. Also, your company needs to contend with cybersecurity and compliance risks.

Vendors can also pose operational risks stemming from changes with its business model.

In 2022, Apple added new user privacy controls to its operating system which threw the online advertising business into disarray. The changes gave users more control over privacy. This made it difficult for advertisers to track ad performance and they pulled back on spending. Facebook parent company Meta Platforms estimated changes to Apple's ad tracking policy would cost the company $10 billion that year. Facebook stock set a record when shares collapsed by 26.4 percent and its market valuation plunged by more than $232 billion. It was the biggest one-day drop in market value for any company in the history of the US stock market.[43]

Periodically assess and review supplier risks to protect your business.

- Identify your most likely and highest-impact risks, and prioritize
- Work with your suppliers to forecast issues, solve potential problems, and minimize impacts

- Diversify your supply chain. Source primary and secondary suppliers to minimize vulnerability points (weather, labor, political,
  or economic events)

─────────── TAKE-AWAYS: ───────────

- Uncover hidden areas of liability. You can't improve what you don't know.
- Identify risk tripwires related to customers, key employees, and suppliers.
- Customers
  - Revenue concentration risk refers to the potential negative impact on a business if a significant portion of its revenue comes from a single customer or industry.
  - Customer satisfaction and acquisition are important for a business because high customer retention rates can lead to increased profits, while a high customer churn rate can be costly for a business.
  - To calculate customer acquisition cost (CAC), divide the total marketing and sales costs for customer acquisition by the total number of customers acquired. To calculate customer churn rate, divide the number of customers lost in a specific time-period by the number of customers at the start of that period.
- Key Employees
  - When planning to sell your business, think about how you can keep key employees in the loop.
  - The buyer isn't only interested in your business's current cash flows but its future performance as well.
  - Without key employees, business continuity will always be in question.
- Suppliers
  - While some degree of risk has always been inherent in vendor relationships, some suppliers present more risk than others.
  - Periodically assess and review supplier risks to protect your business.
- Transferability considerations

- ○ Take an inventory of the assets in your business—tangible and intangible.
- ○ Assess the transferability to determine their value and the potential success of a business sale.
- ○ Minority-owned business certifications and other industry licenses and certifications can be important assets for a business and should be considered when developing a plan for a potential sale.

MY ACTION PLAN

What are some specific ways you plan to reduce risk in your business and improve transferability to a new owner?

Action Item	Resources Needed	Start By Date	Complete By Date

CHAPTER 10

MOST OF YOUR REVENUES ARE ONE-TIME SALES

Progress is impossible without change, and those who cannot change their minds cannot change anything.

GEORGE BERNARD SHAW

I f your revenues are primarily driven by one-time sales, your annual forecast may feel more like a guess than a plan. It can be challenging to know what your revenues will look like next year if you don't have upfront commitments from customers.

One-time revenue models are based on single projects or payments that may or may not happen again. One-time sales can have a higher sense of immediacy and closure compared to recurring revenue.

With a one-time purchase, you don't know when new customers are going to make another purchase, or even if they're likely to purchase again.

Many industries have shifted from a one-time sales model to a recurring revenue model. This allows businesses to generate consistent revenue by providing ongoing access to products or services in exchange for regularly scheduled payments.

Recurring revenue feeds into the predictability of future cash flow. Recurring revenue is an agreement for a customer to buy from you via a scheduled payment or a contract term.

Let's take the example of the automobile industry. Customers can subscribe to cars as a service instead of purchasing outright. Audi, Porsche, and Nissan offer all-inclusive subscriptions—the car, insurance, and maintenance cost combined into a single monthly fee. Unlike in a traditional lease, the customer has the option to easily switch cars during their subscription. The model benefits the car manufacturers by creating an additional channel for predictable income and more quickly adjust to changing customer demands.

Another example is a security services business. The business was doing $1,000,000 in revenue providing installations on a project-basis.

Their business was valued at 0.75 times revenue or $750,000. Over time, they shifted the business to 100 percent monitoring services. With more predictable cash flow and low customer churn, the business value increased to $2 million.

What are different types of recurring revenue business models?

- **Rent**—A contracted payment for a specified time and terms.
- **Hard Contracts**—Phone plans are the best example of hard contracts. When you sign up for a plan, you get a device for free (or a nominal amount). Then you pay a monthly fee to use it. These fixed contracts can range from six months to three years. When the contract period ends, a rolling monthly contract enables you to keep using the service under the same terms. Iron Mountain has multi-year storage contracts with auto renewal options.
- **Product Subscriptions**—The "box subscription" model can be a powerful subscription model. Successful examples include shaving products like Dollar Shave Club, and clothing like Stitch Fix.
- **Content Subscriptions**—A standard subscription service involves customers paying for your product or service on a weekly, monthly, or yearly basis. Netflix has an "all you can eat" content model with access their full catalog paid annually or monthly until you cancel.
- **Support Contracts**—Consider how you might offer a premium version of your support contracts. For example, Salesforce offers a "front of the line" premium level of customer support to shorten wait times.
- **Sunk Money Consumable**—When a customer makes an initial investment into a product that requires further purchases to function properly, it's what John Warrillow, author of *Built to Sell*, calls a "sunk money consumable." Some examples of sunk money consumables: Brita water filter system. If you want clean water, you must keep buying new Brita filters. Nespresso coffee machine. You buy the coffee machine, and to make coffee you need to buy Nespresso coffee capsules.

- **Sunk Money Subscriptions**—Same principle as sunk money consumables. But instead of buying a tangible product, consumers pay for a subscription. Warrillow uses the Bloomberg Terminal as an example of a sunk money subscription. Wall Street traders must buy the platform to receive the intended value—Bloomberg's financial publications.
- **Vendor Lock-in**—this model makes customers dependent on a specific product or service provider. You're not able to change for another provider without incurring a switching cost—meaning you could incur the inconvenience with taking time to switch. The time, effort, and money a customer would have to invest into changing the provider tip the scales so that it's not worth it. If you leave Nextflix, you'll lose your personalized content recommendations. If you leave LinkedIn, you'll abandon all the connections you've gathered over the years.
- **Service Retainers or Subscriptions**—Professionals and service providers can generate guaranteed income by offering retainers. For a recurring monthly fee, the client gets a certain deliverable such as a predefined number of hours, projects or updates completed, or service calls. Financial services firms offer subscriptions for part-time CFO services. Heating and air conditioning HVAC companies offer subscriptions for servicing your equipment.
- **Online Membership**—A membership site to provide valuable content, build a community, and services in a more scalable way compared to one-on-one delivery.

Based on these descriptions, what percent of your total revenue today is recurring (annual contracts, subscriptions, or other written agreements)?

___ 75 percent–100 percent

___ 50 percent–75 percent

___ 25 percent–50 percent

___ 0–25 percent

___ Not sure

There is a difference between recurring and reoccurring revenue. Reoccurring revenue may be likely but less certain. A customer may frequently buy from you without a formal commitment, it can be challenging to know the amount and timetable of their purchases. Reoccuring revenue may be valued differently because there may uncertainty about the transferability of those sales to a new owner. If your customer is on a payment schedule, or renewal is automatic, that is more predictable than someone who doesn't have a contract at all. It is also hard to plan your business around this uncertainty.

What if you were able to create a recurring revenue model in your business? Let's explore how a service can be "productized."

How to Productize Your Service

People buy products that solve a specific problem. This holds true for consumers and business-to-business procurement.

Harvard professor Theodore Levitt shared an excellent analogy: "People don't want to buy a quarter inch drill. They want a quarter inch hole."

The result is a solution to your customers' problems. They will be motivated to spend money to make their lives better.

In his book, *The Automatic Customer*, John Warrillow provides a blueprint for turning your service into a product and building a recurring revenue model around it.

Step 1: Niche Down

Determine which specific market or customer segment to serve. Selecting a niche group will enable you to create products for one type of customer. You'll want to research different aspects of your customer, which might include:

- Demographics (age, gender, income)
- Firmographics (company size, industry, location)

- Life stage (just married, retirement)
- Company life stage (start up, mature)
- Psychographics (attitudes, motivations, values)

If you feel uncomfortable with this step, I understand why. It may seem counterintuitive to narrow your market. Picking one niche helps you focus on the key problems facing your target audience, and ultimately design a product that solves their problems.

To gain additional insight, consider the following questions:

What makes your company tick?
- What is your organization passionate about?
- What are you particularly good at?

What do you know about current or potential customers?
- Why does the customer need or want your company?
- What customer needs or wants are not being met currently?
- Talk with customers in 1x1 interviews, focus groups, surveys, or use 3rd party research to inform your thinking.
- Who are your most profitable customers? What do they have in common?
- Define the potential of your niche segment.

What can you learn about your competition?
- What drives their economic engines?
- What are they known for in the marketplace?

Jane Portman is a user experience consultant and niched down to focus on the owners of small Software-as-a-Service (SaaS) companies. She developed "The UI Audit" product, which packages her user experience consulting into a product.

Other niche market examples include Spanx (targeting 40-60 year old women who have become more concerned with their personal appearance) and Stitch Fix Men (aspirational everyman).

Who is your target market? How can you niche down? (And niche down again?)

_____

_____

_____

Step 2: Discover Your Teachable, Valuable, and Recurring (TVR) Solution

The next step is to categorize the services you offer against three criteria:

- **T**eachable to employees (you can teach others how to deliver the service, and it doesn't need to involve you)
- **V**aluable to your customers (use the niche you selected in step 1)
- **R**ecurring need (how frequently your niche has a need to buy)

Make a list of all the services you offer to your market niche. Then score each service on a scale of 1 (relatively low) to 10 (relatively high). Add up the scores across each row for a combined TVR score.

Current Services	Teachable	Valuable	Recurring	Total

The service that scored highest is: _____

Step 3: Be Clear on Your Quarter Inch Hole

Be clear about what problem your product solves for your niche.

What's for dinner tonight? That question used to stress me out. Typically, my young kids would ask me in the morning when I had a long workday ahead.

According to Food Industry Advisor David Portalatin at The NPD Group, "As late as thirty minutes before dinner there will still be about 18 percent of you who don't know the answer to that question."[44]

What I needed as a working parent was an easy and convenient way to decide what we are having for dinner and make it happen.

Since then, food industry innovators have developed solutions to this problem. Grocery stores offer more ready-to-eat meals with fresh ingredients. Blue Apron and Hello Fresh deliver ready-to-prepare fresh meals to your doorstep. These businesses are cleverly providing a solution to the problem of not knowing what's for dinner.

When you understand the "why" behind what you sell, you'll be able to solve your customers' problems.

What problems does your target market need to solve?

_____

_____

_____

Step 4: Brand Your Product

With a service, you're typically hiring a person. With a product, you're selling a thing. Name your product, then give it a brand name.

Using the "why" from step 3, decide which benefits of your product are most important to the customer. Brainstorm a unique brand name that communicates the product will address their needs.

Rocket Mortgage is a great example conveying the benefit of speed for homebuyers.

The name "Amazon" is a nod to the world's largest river and is meant to represent the company's vast selection and global reach.

HelloFresh's name is memorable and suggests a service for delivering fresh ingredients and easy-to-prepare recipes to customers' doorsteps.

ZipRecruiter's name is descriptive, suggesting a platform for quickly and easily finding job candidates.

Give your process a name:

_____

_____

_____

Step 5: List Your Ingredients

Standardize the process and list what customers get when they buy your product.

Service businesses usually customize their deliverables in a unique proposal for every prospect. In contrast, product companies put their ingredients on the label. Make a list of what customers get when they buy your product.

Many entrepreneurs don't exceed $5 million in revenue because they don't develop repeatable processes to scale the business.

Once you standardize and document your process steps, you can train employees to help them understand their role and provide them with a roadmap to execute.

DataStories.com is an analytics platform that offers a process to generate insights from your data in no time. They are selling a service, made to appear as a product. How does it work?

1. Upload your data
2. Select your target key performance indicator
3. Submit your story
4. Extract valuable insights
5. Communicate results

Kevin Urrutia built a residential apartment cleaning service called Maid Sailors. He and his brother scaled their NYC-based service by standardizing the client quoting process and bundling cleaning packages.

List the ingredients of your process:

_____

_____

_____

_____

_____

_____

Step 6: Preempt Objections

When selling a service, you typically hear your prospect's objections firsthand so you can dynamically address them on the spot.

When selling a product, you don't always have the benefit of personal interaction to overcome objections.

Consider what potential objections you customers might have and preempt them with an FAQ.

Spiffy offers on-demand car care. They address potential objections in their online FAQ including:

- "Are there any services you do not warranty?"
- "What is your policy about vehicle damage?"
- "How are you protecting your employees and my vehicle from COVID-19?"

List potential objections to proactively address:

_____

_____

_____

_____

_____

Step 7: Publish a Price

Services are quoted by the hour, day, or project and usually come at the end of a custom proposal. Products publish their price, which is one reason they feel more tangible. A published price communicates that you have a standard offering that doesn't change for each customer.

Examples of productized services that have been branded and clearly priced:

- Author Tucker Max productized his book launch experience into a company called Scribe, offering a repeatable process for developing a book.
- Bench offers dedicated bookkeeping and tax services with different subscription options. You connect your bank data and they provide income statements and balance sheets each month.

Ideas for how to price your product:

_____

_____

_____

_____

Step 8: Use the Scarcity Principle

The scarcity principle of persuasion coined by Dr. Robert Cialdini means the more difficult it is to obtain a product, the more valuable it becomes. We're more likely to buy when we think the product will be unavailable than if there were no impression of scarcity.

One of the benefits of a service business is that you have sales leverage because your time is scarce. With a product business, where your offering is always available, you need to give people a reason to act today rather than tomorrow.

TOMS shoe company uses the scarcity principle to encourage shopping and philanthropy with limited availability products such as WildAid panda-themed shoe designs.

When Spotify music service first launched, user access was invitation-only. Taking a similar tactic, Clubhouse was invitation-only when the social audio app launched.

Ideas for how to use the scarcity principle:

_____

_____

_____

_____

"How to Productize Your Services"
Andy Cabasso, Co-Founder, JurisPage
Succession Stories Podcast E81[45]

Andy Cabasso co-founded JurisPage, a marketing services company for law firms. In just three years, they were bought by a strategic acquirer for seven-figures. Andy shared how they turned services into a product with fixed deliverables and standardized procedures to build a scalable process.

Laurie Barkman:
When you're talking about your services, you've created a sense that it's a product. Help us understand how you did that and what that meant.

Andy Cabasso:
Ultimately, what the client wants is the product, the website. But things can go off the rails when things are not clearly defined. To make it easy for both the client and for us in terms of delivering that service, we made our web designs fixed products with fixed deliverables. We said, "You will get a website. We have a few different layout options for home pages for you to choose from in terms of inspiration. You can give us feedback on this and this and this. You're going to have a bio page for X number of lawyers based on how many there are at your firm, a contact page, and a blog page." All of these are very fixed deliverables that the client gets with a certain amount of revision rounds. This is the fixed scope.

On the design side, by having a fixed scope, we know the entire process and workflow to expect. We can build our team to work on this workflow. It ensures that we have an assembly line process from start to finish. Nothing is going to go off the rails. We're going to get the client deliverables and get them the website that they're looking for. This way, things don't get stuck because of scope creep. Going beyond what we had agreed to, and what the client had paid for, is a very real thing that can happen.

Having that fixed product for websites, having fixed products for SEO services, or paid search services, was super important to being able to help us grow the business so that we could take on more clients. Everyone would have the same product timelines. We can know where every single client is at every stage of the way. Also, it helped us scale and build our team. By having all these fixed stages with fixed deliverables and knowing what we're doing every stage of the way, we could easily onboard new team members to work at each of these steps.

A lot of work can be project oriented for a one-time fee. You build a website, give it to them, they pay you a couple thousand dollars and then that's it. But *every client of ours was on a recurring monthly service. Whether it was at the very least us hosting their website and providing ongoing support. Every client had some ongoing package and we built up this book of business. With every client, we increased our recurring revenue as well. A web design client wouldn't just be a couple thousand dollars. It would be [that amount] plus an ongoing $100 or more per month. As we got hundreds of clients that increased our recurring revenue. This meant that if I were ever to take a vacation and make zero sales, we would still have revenue coming in, which was a real asset for our business. Our business wasn't just me or our brand. It was our recurring revenue. This was something of value separately."*

TAKE-AWAYS:

- A recurring revenue model can provide a more predictable and stable source of cash flow for your business.
- Recurring revenue is a key driver of enterprise value.
- There are different types of recurring revenue models to consider.
- Recurring revenue models can be found in product and service businesses.
- Service businesses can scale faster by standardizing repeatable processes and training your teams to deliver.

MY ACTION PLAN

What could you do to increase recurring revenue in your business?

Action Item	Resources Needed	Start By Date	Complete By Date

CHAPTER 11

PAST SUCCESS ISN'T COMPETITIVE FOR TOMORROW

There is nothing permanent except change.

HERACLITUS

What if we looked at companies as if they were people? Like people, companies have an age and stage. They experience a lifecycle from birth to death with four stages propelling them from one phase to the next: startup, growth, maturity, and decline.

Management guru Ichak Adizes describes this as a corporate lifecycle, "The fundamental truth that all organizations, like all living organisms, have a lifecycle and undergo very predictable and repetitive patterns of behavior as they grow and develop."

This has relevance to you as the owner of a business who wants to maximize value throughout the life stages of your company. Adizes advises, "Leading an organization through lifecycle transitions is not easy, or obvious. The same methods that produce success in one stage can create failure in the next. Leaders who fail to understand what is needed (and not needed) can inhibit the development of their companies or plunge them into premature aging."

"Enterprising Generations"
Ann Dugan, Founder, Institute for
Entrepreneurial Excellence
Succession Stories Podcast E18[46]

"In general, the second generation is respectful of the founding generation, the first generation. They don't like to rock the boat. They like to make sure that dad or mom, or whoever in that senior generation—founder and leader—are okay with what they're doing. They tend to be risk averse and be caretakers or

placeholders. That's changed in the last seven to ten years where they might be doing work through their college projects or sometimes high school projects saying, I think this is something we could consider or do differently.

In general, a family needs good communication and good collaboration, so no one feels threatened. I used to hear all the time, everything's great. Our profits are great. Revenue is great. Why be the spouting whale? Because what happens is the spouting whale gets harpooned. With some families that goes on for a long time, until there's a big hiccup, like a pandemic, a labor shortage. Then suddenly, the family says maybe we should have been forward planning a little bit stronger or more proactively. I think that's where you see today, families—especially family leaders—looking where innovation is coming from. Because it's not just in their products and services over the last five, seven years. It's in their use of technology. labor pool, and labor activities. As you look at employment today, needs more than just a paycheck. They need to innovate how we market. Every traditional area of business today needs innovation. Smart, strong family businesses get that and are actively involved with it.

One family told me, "We're going to remain a family held, family-owned company for at least until the end of the earth." They must have a way not only to innovate for today, but also prepare the generation for tomorrow because the research is that families typically grow faster than the wealth.

In many languages and cultures, the first generation was the entrepreneurial generation. But what made them strong as a business leader also made them weak. The sense that a successful entrepreneur is not the most democratic or collaborative. They can be aggressive and domineering because they're focused on mission and what they need to do to be successful in today, tomorrow, and next year.

As the next generation was coming into the business, they figured out the way to get along with everybody is to stay below radar. I don't put my head up because it is like whack-a-mole, I get in trouble. They became place keepers rather than dynamic business leaders. By the third generation, the money was starting to run out, the innovation the technology, or personnel, were aging. They weren't paying as much attention to rejuvenating and rethinking where they are.

Ichak Adizes studied hundreds of thousands of companies. What they show is a bell curve of businesses. You have the beginning, the go-go startup years, all of those things that make you strong or kill you off because you've expanded too fast and you've run out of cash. Or you have moved into new products and services where you have no capacity or capabilities and that's caused you to fail.

A lot of things on the way up can derail you, but let's just say you're on that left side of the bell curve. Moving up, you plateau at the top. It doesn't mean you can stay there. You have to think about what's next. If I start my new bell curve, whether it's new markets, regions, products, services, employment, managerial personnel, whatever. I don't want to slide off the right of the bell curve, which is Death Valley, if we don't make some changes.

That's where the third generation inherits or takes over the business when it's really on that right-hand curve sliding downward. All of a sudden, they have a hole to dig out of that they may or may not be prepared to do. If the second generation had done some of the heavy lifting of preparation and thinking more than short-term, much longer term— five, seven, ten years out. Those are things that impacts the statistic today because everyone understands there are no placeholders, there are no place keepers here. We need to continually challenge ourselves."

Recall previous chapters describing the relationship between risk and value in your business. Premature aging can lead to the attributes that can make your business less attractive, less transferable, less sellable—less valuable.

One of the challenges for mature companies is to innovate before it's too late. To seek reinvention through improved business development, marketing, product/services, or processes.

Your mature company has a history of accumulated successes. Over time, it can be still effectively operating and have strong financial statements.

You know there is a "but" coming . . .

But, mature companies can face key challenges, plunging them into decline:

- Become slow, cumbersome, unexciting
- Have reduced expectations for growth
- Lose market share to competitors
- Operating and marketing challenges
- Demonstrate little interest in conquering new markets, technologies, or trends
- Vulnerable as doubts, problems, threats, and internal issues creep in
- Problems overshadow the original mission
- Focused inward on administration

A company that isn't growing is in decline. "Death" occurs when no one remains committed to sustaining the organization.

There are two main types of growth strategies: "Organic" and "Inorganic." Organic growth is achieved by expanding your company's output and internal activities to increase revenue. Inorganic growth comes from mergers, acquisitions, and joint ventures.

Which growth strategy is right for your business depends on the level of investment and risk that you're willing to assume.

Another framework is "build versus buy." Should you invest sales and marketing resources or develop innovations to increase revenue and profits? Or should you acquire an existing company to achieve your growth goals?

Organic Growth vs. Mergers & Acquisitions
Which growth strategy fits your business?

Organic Growth (Build)	Mergers & Acquisitions (Buy)
• Slower paced • More control • Fewer upfront investments • Focuses on core business • Innovations can take company to the next level	• Faster growth, but more risk • New markets, geographies, industries • Bring new assets into portfolio—recognizable brands, intellectual property, capabilities, talent (acqui-hire) • Requires large amounts of capital • Can divert focus from core business • Integration is critical

Innovation Growth Strategy

Innovation can play an important role for well-established companies not only for differentiation but also to ensure the viability of the business for future generations. Research published by Harvard Business Review found that particularly during recessionary times, companies that innovate have a higher chance of surviving the economic downturn and finding themselves in a better competitive position on the other side.[47]

Sean Ammirati is a longtime friend and colleague. He is the Executive Director of The Carnegie Mellon Corporate Startup Lab, an interdisciplinary group focused on researching and promoting the mission of transformative innovation within corporations. I am one of the adjunct professors for the masters-level course. Every semester, I am blown away by the innovative work of the project teams. The core philosophy is that startups can exist and thrive anywhere, including in large corporations and mature companies.

Sean describes four categories of innovation. The matrix evaluates the impact on existing customers versus new customers, and whether we are using existing assets to deliver the innovation or new assets. These categories apply to product, marketing, technological, or process innovations. Innovation categories include:

- **Disruptive innovation**—Introducing new assets to your existing customers to create value. With the iPhone, Apple took existing technology and created a new user experience by replacing buttons with a touch-oriented interface. Netflix introduced a new business model for an existing service for digital streaming.
- **Incremental innovation**—Gradually introducing continuous improvements of your existing assets to your current customers. This is a low-risk way to increase market share of well-established products or services. Your ability to effectively listen to customer feedback will determine success in this arena. Done successfully, you will positively impact customer satisfaction and profits. The small upgrades that phone companies frequently introduce are an example of incremental innovation.
- **Architectural innovation**—Applying existing assets to a new market as a low-risk innovation strategy because you're building on proven success in some areas. Uber and Lyft took existing technology for ridesharing and geolocation and applied it to the transportation industry to create an alternative to taxis. Architectural innovations can increase your competitive advantage by appealing to a wider customer base.
- **Transformational innovation**—Creating an innovation that responds to customers' needs in new ways. It may also create a new industry. The airplane revolutionized travel by creating a new market and new technology that enabled customers to travel long distances faster. In more recent years, Blue Origin and other

space tourism companies are reimagining long distance travel in a whole new light.

Assets

		Existing	New
Markets	**New**	Architectural Innovation	Transformational Innovation
	Existing	Incremental Innovation	Disruptive Innovation

Michael Schoedinger is the sixth generation CEO of his family's funeral and cremation business. Their company was started in 1855. Michael shared great examples how they incorporated societal innovations into their business to cultivate adjacent business opportunities—from horse and buggy to a motorized vehicle, to air conditioning, which was an expensive innovation in those days. A more recent innovation for the company was expanding funeral services for pets. Schoedinger did a market study and interviewed 130 veterinarians; he identified a need for pet owners to express their grief with funeral and cremation services. By listening to the marketplace, Schoedinger created an architectural innovation. It provides a practical example of how to understand what problems or challenges your market is facing and determine what you can do to help innovate and solve those problems.

An Economic Moat Is Your Competitive Advantage

The adage "change is constant" looms large. The pace of new technologies, changing customer preferences, and new market trends, can wreak havoc on companies with a strong history of accumulated successes.

As your company matures through the corporate lifecycle, what worked for your business in the past may not be enough to secure its success in the future.

One of the areas that can help impact your future success is creating an economic moat through competitive differentiation.

For decades, legendary investor Warren Buffet has discussed the importance of having an "economic moat" around your business.

An economic moat is a metaphor that refers to your business being able to maintain a competitive advantage over your competitors to preserve market share and profits. Any method that you use to maintain a competitive edge can be considered an economic moat.

Just like a medieval castle, a moat serves to protect the fortress from outsiders. How likely you are to sustain an onslaught of economic competition is determined by strength of your weapons and artillery—your company's competitive advantages.

To evaluate a company and its economic moat, consider these questions:

1. What are the sources of revenue for the company?
2. Of these revenue sources, which is the cash cow?
3. What is the industry of the company?
4. Who are the competitors in this industry?
5. What is the company doing to stand out from its competitors?

As an example, let's look at Apple's economic moat. Actually they have a few. Their primary moat was innovative product development, creating products that did not exist before putting music and computers into our hands with the iPod, iPhone, and iPad. Over time, Apple's strong economic moat is dominated by its brand, customer experience, marketing, and design.

How to Create an Economic Moat

There are several ways to create an economic moat and gain advantage over your competitors.

Cost Advantage

Do you have any cost advantages that competitors cannot replicate? As a company achieves economies of scale, it can produce each unit for less than it could before, meaning that it can charge less for that product in the marketplace, which would attract customers and undercut competitors.

Size Advantage

Does your company have economies of scale through a size advantage? More units of a good or service can be produced on a larger scale with lower overhead costs such as financing, advertising, production, etc. Smaller players are forced to leave the industry or embrace smaller "niche" roles.

High Switching Costs

Would your suppliers or customers incur a high switching cost to do business with a competitor? Competitors can have a difficult time winning "sticky" relationships because of significant switching costs.

Intangibles

Does your company have intangible assets? Refer to the list you created in Chapter 7. Intangible assets include patents, brand recognition, government licenses, and others. Strong brand name recognition allows these types of companies to charge a premium for their products over other competitors' goods, which boosts profits. Innovation initiatives that create competitive advantages are an excellent way to stay ahead of the competition.

Management and Culture

Does your company have an exceptional management or a unique corporate culture? A unique leadership and corporate environment may contribute to a firm's economic success through talent retention. This is particularly important for industries susceptible to the Great Resignation or Quiet Quitting economic trends in which employees have voluntarily resigned from their jobs en masse, beginning in early 2021 in the wake of the COVID-19 pandemic.

Karen Norheim is the second-generation president of American Crane & Equipment Corporation, a specialized manufacturing company in Pennsylvania, founded by her father. What stood out to me during our conversation was how she is approaching innovation as a differentiator. In early 2020 at the start of the COVID-19 pandemic, American Crane launched an innovation lab for digital transformation technologies like IoT and virtual reality. Karen described her philosophy of crawl, walk, run as a framework for launching new technologies and how their innovation culture helps them differentiate.

"Next Gen Corporate Innovation"
Karen Norheim, President and COO, American Crane
Succession Stories Podcast E50[48]

"We created the lab, bought several different—I call them toys—they're not really toys. Yes, they are cool, but they are things that can bring us business outcomes. I put a team together and said here's your funding, here's what I want you to do. You go figure it out. Here's your sandbox, here's your whitespace. I'm not going to tell you which project to go after. I'm just going to say you've got my support, and you've got my funding. Now you smart engineers who are way smarter than me, go forth, figure it out and come back to me. I'm just a sherpa for people who are far more brilliant.

My goodness, it worked so well. What they're coming back with is just incredible. I thought some of the things would take much longer. The speed at which they're going, the energy that's happening is great. If you have amazing people, whatever industry you're in, if you can create an area with a sandbox experience for R&D, innovation, and find things that work. Wonderful things can happen and that's your job as a leader to cultivate."

How Innovation and Differentiation Impact Business Value

Consider when a potential buyer of your company is evaluating your business. If they are significantly larger than your business (per the 5-20 Rule) questions they will likely discuss privately amongst themselves is whether they can replicate what you do. Can they offer your products and services, or switch over your customers, in a cost-effective and efficient way? Or, will they gain competitive advantage by acquiring your company's economic moat attributes.

From a buyer's view, it is ideal to invest in growing companies as they begin to reap the benefits of a wide and sustainable economic moat.

The longevity of the moat is a critical factor.

The longer a company can harvest profits, the greater the benefits for itself and its shareholders. If your company is on the tail-end of that lifecycle, it will have a lower value to buyers or investors. Companies with a strong economic moat enjoy higher valuations. Multi-generational businesses can benefit from innovation initiatives evoking your entrepreneurial roots.

─────────────── **TAKE-AWAYS:** ───────────────

- A company's lifecycle consists of four stages: startup, growth, maturity, and decline. Recognizing what stage a company is in, and understanding the challenges it may face, can be important for maximizing value and planning a transition strategy.

- Companies that are not growing are in decline. Determine whether organic growth or M&A strategies are a fit for your business.

- An economic moat is a competitive advantage that helps a company maintain market share and profits. It can be evaluated by looking at a company's sources of revenue, its cash cow, its industry, its competitors, and its efforts to stand out from those competitors.

- Factors that can contribute to a company's economic moat include brand recognition, a large customer base, network effects, cost advantages, and regulatory barriers. Companies with strong economic moats may be more attractive to potential buyers and may command higher valuations.

- Innovation is not only for only startups. Mature companies can develop product, market, and process innovations to increase profits, customer satisfaction, and enhance your competitive differentiation.

--- **MY ACTION PLAN** ---

What can you do to enhance or create an economic moat and competitive differentiation in your business?

Action Item	Resources Needed	Start By Date	Complete By Date

CHAPTER 12

CONSIDERING FAMILY OR MANAGEMENT SUCCESSION

I'm not saying I'd make a better CEO. That's unsaid.

CONNOR ROY ON THE HBO SERIES, SUCCESSION

This quote comes from the high stakes TV drama about the fictional Roy family and their incessant quest for power. While the family patriarch lays unconscious in the hospital, the siblings debate who to name as CEO in the meantime to avoid a stock market crash. The eldest sibling Connor, often left out of the power moves, 'unsays' that he's a better candidate than his younger and more talented brother, Kendall. But as Kendall points out, "It's not unsaid if you say it."

In drama and in real life, it's better to have a plan than no plan. In your plan, it's also better to have more than one option. Not only to avoid Roy style conflict but because sometimes our plans change.

When time is on your side, when you can generate different options and take the time to explore them. That that's why I advocate for starting sooner than you think you might want to. You need time to hire and invest in your replacement.

A business needs to be independent of its owner, so the business can continue without them. Do you want your family or key managers to take over the business? Maybe the question to ask is whether they want to do that?

One summer I was working with a client on his exit plan. His goal was to step back from the day-to-day operations of the business and focus on relationship and community building. His ideal exit path was to sell the business to his "2IC" second-in-command manager over the next five to seven years.

I asked my client whether his 2IC was interested owning the business one day. "I'm not sure," he said. "I am intending to discuss with him at the end of the year." When the time came to have the discussion, the tables turned. Instead of my client leading the conversation with his vision, the 2IC manager opened with his big news. He decided to move overseas and wanted to work remotely for the next few years with his US-based team and clients. Those plans went out the window. It's a good reminder not to put all your eggs in one basket, because you just never know.

Succession Planning Versus Exit Planning

A succession plan is different from an exit plan. A succession plan is used to identify who the key employees are in the business, typically the owner and a few key other employees.

You can use a succession plan to determine who is going to succeed you in operating the business one day.

Having a transferable business means that your business cannot be 100 percent dependent on you. To have a seamless transition from the business, you will need to have a succession of leadership and determine who will be running the business in the future.

When you're thinking about who to transition your company to, you may assume it is your management team.

In my first meeting with a client, he told me his intention to sell his manufacturing business to his operational supervisors. Our conversations about the business and its financial challenges helped him see how employees took a narrower view. Envisioning how they would operate the business as owners was too big of a hurdle to overcome.

Author and succession planning consultant, Beth Armknect Miller (Succession Stories Podcast E74) suggests: "The first step is to analyze what the gaps are. You need to understand what your key positions are versus the key people and determine, 'Okay, are those key people in the key positions?' If so, what are those skills or behaviors that need to be developed, so that they're ready in time for that next position?"

How do you make sure that you can identify your high potentials, and make sure that you're developing them in a timely manner, so that they're prepared. There's a lot of research, especially with millennials, that if they're not getting developed, they're going to leave.

The idea of a succession plan, if you can communicate that you've got a succession plan in your organization, you don't have to—you're not naming names—you're just saying, "Hey, we are committed to a succession plan, which means developing the people within the organization to be ready for when our company is larger, to take on more responsibilities." You're not committing to stepping away, you're committing to your employees, and developing them.

If the employees know that there's a succession plan, and that they're being developed as part of that plan, you're more likely to retain them and retain them for a longer period of time."

Family Succession

Most businesses fail to stay in business. You may have been surprised by the statistics in an earlier chapter about company longevity. Only 35 percent of all companies make it to their tenth birthday. The most common reasons businesses don't continue are due to things out of our control.

Businesses can cease operations when the owner dies or is disabled, a key employee leaves, the business loses a critical customer or vendor, or there are disagreements between owners, business partners, or family members. Or because the business is struggling. If your family sees that your company is struggling, would they want to be part of it? Does your family want it? If so, they must be a fit, have the right skills, and be motivated.

Daniel Van Der Vliet is the executive director of the Smith Family Business Initiative at Cornell University to strengthen and support family businesses. Daniel shared ways family businesses can involve the next generation in succession planning and future of their businesses.

"Changing the Family Business Narrative"
Daniel Van Der Vliet, Cornell Univ.
Smith Family Business Initiative
Succession Stories Podcast E80[49]

Laurie Barkman:
How do we make it more objective for the next generation coming in a position of strength as an individual?

Daniel Van Der Vliet:
This is a very important aspect for family businesses because there are a lot of unwritten rules. A lot of implicit actions we take are based sometimes on gender, birth order, on the family itself. When those get rolled into the family business, they can be dangerous if the oldest, or first son always becomes the CEO. I love to use this example of a business in Vermont, how they tackled this. The business was four brothers, and they created a series of rules, almost like a constitution, on a piece of notebook paper. They all agreed that the next generation needed to get an education. They did not stipulate what that education was, just that the education itself was valuable for the individual. Ultimately, the business was not here to serve the individual, the individual was there to serve the business. Two, to go get outside experience. It could be in a similar type of industry but that was not stipulated. The underscore was that experience matters. If you don't end up back at the family business, you need to succeed on your own. The third was returning to the business if they so choose. They would have to work for one of the other brothers and you would not come into a position immediately and work for your dad, and then succeed him that easily. You had to see how other parts of the business worked and then eventually, opportunities of leadership will be opened to you if you proved successful.

I love that example because it was simple. It was probably done around a kitchen table in one night. It was the fact that they codified these rules, shared them, and they all agreed to them. That's what is ultimately important. It's not just mom or dad making these decisions and not sharing them openly. There was buy-in across all the families and then it made sense. Those rules can be more formal. Some families have family constitutions, and they go much more in detail, but the process by which I think the family arrives at those rules for at least stipulations for employment are very important. Rather than when Junior knocks on the door we're just going to give them a job because their last name is the same.

Laurie Barkman:
What would be some of the keys for a family firm to put someone in place very purposefully, as a "disruptive successor" to quote Jonathan Goldhill?

Daniel Van Der Vliet:
It's important for the next generation to come in and make their mark. This is a challenge. Most successors' biggest fear is that the business will fail on their watch. To come in and make disruptive changes can be daunting, because if those changes don't pan out, then the burden of the family ends up on that person's shoulders.

There was a business founded by two brothers. They had a private label in the skincare space and the business was not doing well. The son of one of the fathers came in and took over.

This is a dramatic example so I am not saying this should be the way everyone approaches it. I do think it exemplifies a way for a successor to come in and say, "This is my business now." In this case, the successor came in and told everybody, they effectively needed to reapply for their jobs. That this was a different company, and we need to take it in a very different direction. He had numbers to justify that. Some people thought, "Yeah, that's great, we can finally get rid of some of the dead wood around here." But the successor was clear that it meant everybody. I don't know how many people were hired back, but I do know many of them were. The message was, "This is not my father's company anymore. This is my company, and this is the direction I'm seeking to take this in."

It paid off greatly. Today the company is still growing under that individual's leadership. It takes bold moves and the confidence to make them. In this case what was important, was the individual had been out of the family business for ten to fifteen years and had a successful career. It underscores the value of outside experience, and not coming back to the business just because your family owns it, and you're instantly seated as the vice president waiting to be the CEO. Outside experience is key, and be bold in those situations.

Jonathan Goldhill has been advising closely held and family businesses for over three decades. Drawing from his experience as a strategist and consultant, he is also the author of *Disruptive Successor: A Guide for Driving Growth in Your Family Business.*

"Next Generation Disruptive Successor" Jonathan Goldhill, The Goldhill Group Succession Stories Podcast E110[50]

Laurie Barkman:
We've talked a lot about the third generation, how difficult in the US it is to get to the third and beyond. One of my guests said that spouting whales get harpooned. That theme has recurred enough times that I wanted to ask you about your observations of family dynamics when it comes to the next generation saying, "I've got the keys. I want to innovate, do something different." Does the parent generation give them the freedom to do that, or do they hold back and say, "Now, don't screw it up."

Jonathan Goldhill:
If you're going to transition a business to the next generation, then you have to treat that next generation, whether it's family, or not family, even if you're going to sell the business or pass it along, you have to look at that business from an outside perspective. You have to make yourself indispensable to the company. That is just like the hardest thing for a lot of entrepreneurs to do, because an entrepreneur, at least these types of entrepreneurs, created it not with the idea

that they're going to build it to sell, they built it to create a certain amount of freedom in their lives. They built it around themselves and their abilities and capabilities and they maybe don't have a lot of trust in people. Not trusting people means they can't let go. This trust extends not just to their employees, but it extends to their family members that he or she is going to make the right decisions.

Part of the challenge, Laurie, is that generally it is the predecessor's money that the successor is gambling with. Most of that is the predecessor's business, money, and assets. How many parents do you know that are willing to say to their kids, "Okay, you manage my money?"

The thirty-year old who has a long runway ahead of them in terms of life, they'll bet the farm much more quickly than a person who is sixty, who's looking at retirement. They need to take care of their mortgage for the next fifteen or twenty years while they're remaining. Their risk tolerances are very different and that's part of what makes it challenging. I think it's risk tolerance, but ego and control probably play an even bigger part in why businesses don't transition to the next generation, or at all.

The topic of family businesses comes up frequently on my podcast. Next gen leaders talk about starting at the bottom, sweeping floors, stuffing envelopes. They've worked elsewhere, and then come back to their family business. By doing so, they've earned credibility with their colleagues because people see the value they've added along the way.

Sometimes leadership motivations evolve. Kent Johnson is the fourth-generation CEO of *Highlights*. He told me a story how he was approached by the Family Board, but positively did not want to work in the company. He has been a successful CEO at *Highlights* for more than ten years. He's been a fantastic fit for them and aligned his motivations with the company from a sustainability standpoint, thinking about the future beyond himself.

"Sustainable Innovation"
Kent Johnson, CEO, Highlights
Succession Stories Podcast E40[51]

"Our focus in succession within the family is about engagement with the mission of the company. It's about promoting group stewardship for good governance and for the mission and dream of the founders. We don't presume. Maybe we have people who want to get involved in governance or as employees in the fifth generation. What we really focus on is trying to have as many people as engaged as possible in stewardship. I want to transmit the stewardship that I inherited. I want to be seen as just one of the continuum. That would be the best legacy in terms of the company.

One of the things I think a lot about which I would be very proud to have been my legacy is figuring out how the mission and the values associated with the company become irreversibly part of the culture. I spend time thinking about how to make a culture for a company that doesn't depend on individuals, that will be self-sustaining. We've been through tragedies, and I am very passionate about what we do. I talk to people inside and outside the company passionate about our mission. I recognize someday I won't be able to do that. How do we create a way that more and more people can be part of it and speak with passion and can sustain it? If we can build it into the culture, we can be invincible. If it requires specific individuals, we're always at risk."

"Creating the Family Enterprise of the Future"
Nikè Anani, Next Gen Advisor
Succession Stories Podcast E102[52]

Nikè is an international succession specialist and legacy planning expert for future-focused business families. Nikè works with families to co-create the businesses of the future that they envision.

Laurie Barkman:

We have only so much time on this planet, and 100 percent of business owners are going to leave their company one day. If we don't have these conversations, there can be some fallout. Have you worked with clients or from your own experiences, if you don't address these things while everyone is in the room, proverbially speaking or literally in the room, that there's a real downside here?

Nikè Anani:

Unfortunately, I have. I had a case where a founder had built up a conglomerate of different businesses in different industries. He set up a trust and the scope were the businesses as well as the family foundation. He didn't have any conversations with his spouse or the kids. When he transitioned, he left his spouse and four kids—two were married with children. All four kids and the wife were supposed to be the beneficiaries of the trust and take strategic decisions over the family assets. But only one of the kids had experience working in one of the family businesses.

Also the structure was quite complex. There were a lot of interdependencies between various operating businesses, and there had never been a reporting mechanism in terms of providing financial reports to the shareholders. It was all very informal when Dad was in the room and the siblings were all very different. They'd never worked together. They'd never come into partnership before. Mom also didn't have business expertise so taking strategic decisions together was a bit of a nightmare. They were squabbling in meetings and it was threatening not only the survival of the partnership, but also their family relations.

It got to the point where two of the kids were not turning up for family events like Christmas. That was a real worst-case scenario, where it got to the point where they tried to pull me into the room to improve things. But two of the family members were not willing to cooperate with their family members anymore. It's important that when we take a step back as business founders, we invest in the technical—talk to your attorneys, draw up trusts and wills. You must have these conversations. You must get into a cadence of articulating the vision, and the mission, and the values of the family and starting to co-create. It's important that the siblings start practicing their partnership during the lifetime of the founder, where they understand each other's personalities, perspective, priorities, preferences, and get into a cadence and a rhythm of working together because they're moving from being just siblings to being business partners. Sometimes, like in this case, only one sibling had the expertise for one of the businesses. Sometimes they need time to train and coach and guide them in different elements of corporate governance or industry specific experiences, or softer skills, leadership and influence navigating family dynamics, conflict management and resolution. These things do take time to develop, so it's important to invest in the relational not just the technical.

You may have a child that you would like to see in the business. What if they don't have the skillset or interest in owning the business? It can be disappointing to find out that Junior does not share your vision, especially if you thought that he would be your preferred Exit Plan Option. Depending on your timeline, you may decide to sell the company to a third-party because the next gen option isn't a go.

Or maybe Junior will run the company, but there can be ten to twenty years until that time. Junior may not have the skills or interest. Or it's a time sensitivity where we just can't wait that long to see what happens.

Sometimes there can be a skip generation leadership solution to bridge the readiness gap of the next generation. When the second-generation owner of manufacturing company started to have health issues, they hired in a CEO from the outside to bridge the gap until his two thirty-something sons were ready to assume executive leadership positions. The CEO was hired to grow the business and increase profitability. The two sons had the interest and talents; they needed mentorship and experience. Twenty years later they are running the business as the third-generation leadership. It's a great example of long-term succession planning in a family business.

If you do decide to sell the business to a family member, rather than gift or transfer equity ownership over time (as discussed in the next section), be sure to seek advice from an attorney. For a family succession involving outside funding, you'll want to understand the risk factors. If you are open to "being the bank" and funding the transaction through seller financing, you need to understand the risks you're taking and how long it'll take to get paid back. What happens if the business is not performing? Do you take it back? Work with an attorney to make sure that you're as protected as possible.

Remember, just because someone's related to you doesn't mean that they're rightly qualified.

Internal Transactions / Management Succession

Developing your 2IC and key employees means that you can step aside as needed. Don't view this as a negative. After all, a business that cannot thrive without its owner is a worthless entity.

Have you considered transitioning ownership in your business to your management team?

As you evaluate exit options, consider your feelings toward your key employees or management team. Have they been loyal to you, sticking with you through thick and thin?

A lot of times when people say they want to sell their company it's common to look to the management team first before we look outside.

Why? Because they already know the company. They know all the warts, the risks . . . and want the opportunity. Which means they are motivated to grow in the business.

I spoke with a franchise catering company whose owner intends to sell to his head chef. It's very exciting because he knows the business. He has been part of the success to-date and has demonstrated an owner's mindset by increasing profitability on the menu and operational improvements.

Selling to management may not necessarily bring the highest price. But it will likely bring a fair price.

An exit option you may consider is an indirect acquisition. It is a way to transfer the business to your key employees even if they do not have financial resources or deep pockets to purchase the stock from you outright.

Attorney Michael Silverman explains an indirect acquisition this way:

"We're going to grant a small percentage of the stock in the company to the key employees and put them on a long-term vesting schedule. In essence, they are extremely motivated to grow the value of the business and to see you exit from the business. The first step is that we grant maybe 5 percent of the value of the business to the key employees subject to maybe a ten-year vesting schedule. Then we have a shareholder agreement between the key employees and the owner which says that over time, the owner has the right to re-acquire the company to buy his or her shares. As those shares are being purchased by the company, the shareholders (key employees) are not paying any money for those shares. They're just contributing sweat equity to the business to create cash flow to buy out the owner. As the owner gets redeemed or purchased by the company, the key employees go from owning 5 percent to 20 percent, eventually 100 percent. They're extremely motivated to be able to acquire a company without spending $1 out of their own pocket. The owner is similarly happy because they get to transition the business to their key employees. Key employees are motivated to generate the cash flow to buy the owner out."[53]

Benefits of an internal transaction versus third-party sale:

- Avoid indemnification liabilities
- Key employees know the business inside and out which can remove the element of uncertainty from the purchase price
- Owners should get 100 cents on the dollar
- Owners incur closing costs and professional fees

Depending on your goals, structuring a management succession may be a good way to:

- Continue the culture and legacy you've built
- Ensure employees are treated fairly after you sell

- Ensure continuity of key personnel in the business
- Maintain your brand name or family identity
- Achieve an exit and succession plan that meets all your goals

How to Hire Your Replacement

Maybe your longer-term plan to build a transferable business includes hiring a CEO to run your business day-to-day while you maintain your equity in your business.

Envision coming into the office at ten in the morning and getting a briefing on the business. You put your feet up on the desk and say, "Sounds great, thanks!"

"CEO Succession and Letting Go"
Bruce Walton, Of Counsel at Battalia Winston
Succession Stories Podcast E29[54]

Battalia Winston is one of the world's largest woman-owned executive search firms. Bruce Walton shared his insights on CEO succession and outside hires.

Laurie Barkman:
What are some things that multi-generational companies, who don't have a family member to transition to, should consider when they're looking for a non-family CEO?

Bruce Walton:
Once you're north of $25 or $30 million dollars (in revenue), I think the most important thing for setting the foundation for a successful search is having a board—an outside perspective, a sounding board to help ownership go forward. One of the keys in the smaller company range is that if you bring in a good person from the outside, they're going to bring ideas that may scare the pants off the owner. The owner needs a way to reflect on those ideas and assess them.

The extra perspectives that come from an advisory board are helpful there. The other side of that coin is that a good CEO does not want to be simply at the whim of an owner. They want to have a way to influence the owner. There is some risk management involved here for the outside CEO, protecting them from an owner's whims. A review by a board can get things on track. Owners frequently are emotional about what they're doing. Emotions drive a lot of decisions.

Laurie Barkman:

If a CEO is starting to think about a transition, how many years out should they start having this conversation with themselves or their family?

Bruce Walton:

There's time and there's age. I think it takes at least two or three years for a new board to get its feet on the ground, get its processes in order, and get into a cadence and a comfort zone. I think if you're looking at retiring as a CEO, and you haven't started making plans or thinking about it in your early sixties, it gets harder as you get older. If you reach seventy, without having pulled a trigger here, you may end up going out with your boots on, and that's not good for the enterprise. Frankly, one of the most important jobs a board does is select a new CEO. We've got lots of scar tissue from CEOs who wanted to do the process themselves. We've had to wrestle them back into making sure there's a search committee that has the board involved. It takes time and it takes energy, and you don't just do it on the fly.

Laurie Barkman:

A board can be extremely helpful in being independent and having a broader perspective, especially if they are independent. They're not owners. I'm curious, in your experience. When you talk with the CEO who is the primary owner, and they don't have a family successor, what's the thought process for them in letting go. What's a typical conversation look like in the getting started phase?

Bruce Walton:

I was asked a question by a very successful founder/owner, who said, "What are the five most important things for a successful transition to a non-family CEO?" There were four items I've been talking about and writing about for years. I called a successful CEO who had been in the saddle for ten years and then kicked up to Chair in a search I did quite a few years ago, and he added the fifth item. There's a combination of structures and processes and mindset.

I think that from the structure side, you need board governance, and you need some long-term incentives, so that the new CEO has a clear way to build personal capital and retire when they want to retire. Private family-owned companies are very reluctant to give up stock. They don't have to do that. There are ways to do that on a cash basis in a way that makes the new CEO act and feel like an owner, but without giving up stock. So those are two structural things.

I think the focus on, "Who's going to be successful?" really comes down to fit. There are two components to the word "fit," something that everybody uses as a key term. But what does it really mean? One part of it is culture. Will the CEO embrace and become a steward for the core values of the family? That's an important starting point because they do become the steward of that culture. Stewardship is perhaps the single term that reflects all the things that go into being a successful non-family CEO.

The second piece of fit is what we call competency. Can they do the job? Do they have the skills and experience? We require that our clients go through a process where we identify the top five to seven competencies that you'd like to see displayed successfully in the recent past within the experience by the candidate as a marker that they can come do that for us.

There are two or three documents that come out of the first part of the search. One is a specification. It's a job description, but it's more of a marketing document. It describes the company, what needs to get done, the qualifications, and a little bit about compensation without revealing too much.

Out of that we derive a competency model based on, "If this is the mission and what has to get done, what competencies would you like to see displayed?" They could be things like strategic assessment, very high EQ, financial savvy, strategic hiring—those kinds of things. They're unique to each situation. The top-level descriptions may travel from search to search, but the underpinning (verbiage) that applies to this client is unique to each situation.

The competency model is absolutely core in my view, because once you identify all the important things, then you can ask, "What are the top three or four, and what are the ones where you could give up a little on?" The "nice to have" versus the "must haves" really helps us go into the marketplace. We can talk a little bit about how we do that.

We seek advice from people who know the fish ponds we're fishing, we have about two minutes or less in order to focus their attention on what's really important in this situation. We have to be very much on the same page with our client. The discussions about the competency model and the prioritization of it are absolutely core to getting it done right the first time.

Laurie Barkman:
Do candidates ask about, in a gentle and professional way, the CEO's desires to step back, truly, and separate from the day-to-day?

Bruce Walton:
They do. It's the single most generally asked question. When I want to take on a search, I talk to people within the company. I need to understand the culture from the recruiter's perspective. And at the CEO level, the question always is, "Will they let go?" I can tell a story about a $100 million family business that had a five person outside board. It had a family council. It was very well consulted-to by leaders in the family business consulting arena. But they had a youngest of three brothers who ran the company, each in turn, who had a real control, psychological issue, if you will, and we talked about it. We set up things, like a search committee where there was an outside board member as co-head of the search committee. Once the candidate was appointed, we made sure that

there was an outside lead director to who could talk on behalf of the outside directors.

But interestingly, there was so much concern from the way this CEO had operated that the family council, in conjunction with the board, set up tripwires saying, "If you don't step back and let the new guy do their job and you keep fiddling with things and getting down into management, those tripwires could result in you being thrown off the board." And guess what? Within a year and a half, he was thrown off the board.

If you look, five years ahead, hopefully, the company is going to be larger than it is today. "A" players aren't going to sign into a job that's just going to keep the company where it is. You're really hiring somebody to do a job bigger than the one you have, today. That may be a hard concept to get your head around as a CEO, but you really should be looking "up" at the new CEO candidates, not down. If you're looking down at them, that means they're already smaller than you. And it's a higher risk that they're not going to be the person to take the company to the next level and grow it. I think it's important, and it comes along with respect and rapport, that the mindset be one of thinking five years ahead, "What are we going to need then? And how are we going to get there?" That usually means hiring somebody who's more senior, perhaps, than you had imagined. So you're looking at least across, and probably up, to the candidates.

TAKE-AWAYS:

- Begin CEO succession planning to evaluate competencies of internal candidates or inform an external search process.
- Have thoughtful conversations with key employees or family members about their interests in acquiring the business, don't assume they are!
- For next generation family successors, determine mutual expectations, fit, and norms for coming into the business.

MY ACTION PLAN

How will you approach succession with family or key managers?

Action Item	Resources Needed	Start By Date	Complete By Date

CHAPTER 13

PROCESS OF SELLING THE BUSINESS IS UNFAMILIAR

The great thing in this world is not so much where
we are but in what direction we are moving.

OLIVER WENDELL HOLMES

As an entrepreneur, you're good at running and building your company. You've probably surrounded yourself with talent to help you along the way. It's just as important to realize that you'll want to have the right advisors support your exit, no matter which succession path you choose. Is it possible to sell your business on your own? Maybe.

You may be able to sell your business on your own if:

- You have sold a business in the past and are familiar with the process. You may know what to expect and may be prepared to handle the selling process directly with the buyer.
- You are selling your business to family or employee(s).
- You have ongoing relationships with professional advisors who have experience selling businesses such as an M&A attorney and certified public accountant (CPA).
- If the buyer(s) are qualified and can navigate financing.
- You are prepared to dedicate time to the process.

It may still make sense to hire an experienced intermediary, but if you are in these situations, you may be able to navigate the sale of your business on your own. But why leave the opportunity to chance?

It's common to focus on the top-line—the price a buyer offers to pay you for the business. The amount you take home after taxes is the real story. If you are working on a transaction without an intermediary, make sure you have a firm grasp of the tax implications of your sale.

M&A advisors will work with your accountant upfront to devise a tax minimization strategy to achieve the best possible outcome. By negotiating and structuring your sale correctly, an experienced intermediary or M&A advisor can help save you tens of thousands of dollars. An accounting firm, M&A attorney, and financial advisor, can also provide value throughout the process to help you maximize net proceeds from the sale and minimize risk to you.

Why Work With an M&A Advisor?

The role of an M&A advisor is to find a buyer and negotiate the sale of the business to achieve your financial objectives. Advisors understand that your priority and expertise is running your business. They serve as your "quarterback" from buyer development to closing. Additionally they will collaborate with your legal and tax advisors to help protect your interests in a transaction.

One of my clients was trying to determine why should he hire an M&A advisor. He spoke with another business owner who told him, "They're providing a level of service on things that you just wouldn't want to be doing. It's very different from running your business day-to-day." He shared this story because he appreciates all of the work that's happening behind the scenes on his behalf.

Here are five reasons to consider working with an M&A advisor:

1. **A misconception is that selling your company on your own will save you money.**

I've spoken with entrepreneurs who sold their businesses on their own and have lingering doubts. Would they have had a better outcome if they had worked with an M&A intermediary?

Here's a question—which of the following describes your biggest fear when it comes to selling your business?

*   Not getting the value I think my business is worth

- That the legacy that I've built will not continue, or will change from what I like it to be
- That I would disappoint my employees
- That no one can run things as well as I can
- Not having anything to do in retirement

The most common answer I see in the workshops that I lead with executive groups across the United States is the first one: "Not getting the value I think my business is worth."

Working with an M&A intermediary gives you the greatest chance of getting the best price and terms. A qualified intermediary, or M&A advisor, will provide value that far exceeds their commission—from creating competition amongst qualified buyers, securing deal terms, and representing your interests all the way through the process. Overall, a benefit is having the peace of mind that you did everything you could to maximize the sale.

If you sell your company on your own, you may underestimate the time it will take to manage the entire process (and how it will distract you from your running your company). There are hundreds of steps to complete along the way.

Often owners ask their attorney or CPA to assist. Caution: you may end up paying more for services. Services are more cost effectively provided by an M&A firm or business broker, and it might take longer if the attorney or CPA don't perform this type of work regularly.

"Selling Your Company"
John Warrillow, Author of The *Built to Sell* Trilogy, and Founder of The Value Builder System
Succession Stories Podcast E82[55]

John Warrillow may be a familiar name if you've read his books or listened to Built to Sell Radio. Prior to starting The Value Builder System, John started and exited four companies.

Laurie Barkman:

When it comes to selling their business, how effective is it for owners to do on their own?

John Warrillow:

I'm reminded of Arik Levy which really demonstrates the before and after of whether to use an M&A professional or not. Arik started a similar business in a similar industry. The first one was called Laundry Locker where they put these lockers and locker mats for people who had to pick up their laundry after hours. He'd built it up and decided he wanted to sell it and didn't want to hire an M&A professional. He thought he could do it himself. He went around trying to sell the business for months, but couldn't get an offer. Eventually he got a single offer. He agreed to it, they signed a non-binding letter of intent with a no-shop clause so he gave up all his negotiating leverage trying to sell to anybody else. He went through sixty days of due diligence in good faith and on the last day of due diligence, the very last minute, the acquirer comes and says, "We were going to buy this company for x, we've looked at it and now we think it's worth 20 percent less than x."

What Arik didn't realize at the time was he had been re-traded on. This was illegitimate re-trading. It was them, locking him into a letter of intent, not creating competitive tension, and then effectively lowering the price because they knew they could. They knew they had him over the ropes and he threw his arms up and slammed his fist down, but agreed to the lower price. Then only days later, did they reveal that they didn't have the money to buy the business and that even though the value is lower, the only way they could consummate the deal is if Arik himself financed the deal. In other words, letting them buy the business over the years and it was a terrible outcome.

Arik skinned his knees and licked his wounds and got back into the same business. This time it was a company called Luxer One. They put lockers into different Manhattan apartment buildings and it became a very successful business. This time Arik went to sell and hired an M&A professional. They ran a process. He put a CIM [Confidential Information Memorandum] together professionally. Arik got eight offers, all of which were plus or minus 10 percent the original round. That's when his Advisor earned his commission because he went to the eight potential acquirers and said, "You've got to do better," and played one off the other. In the end, Arik got three times more than the average initial offer."

2. Most owners sell a business only once in their lifetime.

M&A advisors have been through the process of selling businesses many times. So an advisor is well-positioned to manage challenging aspects of the process as they come along. They quarterback the process, handling communications with buyers, lenders, and keeping things moving forward in a strategic manner.

If you sell on your own, you'll end up spending hundreds of hours on buyer inquiries, vetting, calls, meetings, negotiating deal terms, and responding to due diligence.

Recognize that "time kills deals"—having an advisor handle the process with time sensitivity is a key aspect of getting across the finish line to closing.

This enables you to stay focused on your business. The reality is that selling your business can be a distraction. You don't want to take your eye off the ball while you're selling your business. If revenues and profits decline, buyers and lenders get nervous wondering when, or if, things will turn around.

Even with an advisor, it is common for business owners to get caught up in the emotions of selling your business. No one wants to hear that their baby is ugly. Imagine your facial expression if you receive an offer that's lower than you might expect. It can be painful. Advisors serve as an emotional buffer to potentially derailing situations.

3. Advisors create buyer competition to ensure you get the best deal.

The merger and acquisition (M&A) firm you choose should provide a detailed roadmap for marketing your business.

The selling process outlined below provides detail on a typical process used with clients.

An advisory firm will develop a written description of your company called a Confidential Information Memorandum (CIM). The CIM describes your business strategy, market, products/services, financials, team, differentiation, and reasons for sale. A CIM is typically twenty to forty pages long. Also, potential buyers don't receive the CIM until they have executed a non-disclosure agreement. Maintaining confidentiality is crucial throughout the process.

Working with an M&A advisor may provide the opportunity to create competitive demand amongst potential buyers. You'll have a better chance of finding a buyer that's a great fit under the best possible price and terms.

4. Advisors manage the selling process from start to finish.

Here are the major steps in the selling process and brief description of each.

Process Step	Description	Month
1—Data Gathering (Pre-M&A Diligence)	• Collect financials, lease information, and other pre-diligence information • Develop a business valuation • Define process and timeline for buyers • Timeline to completion: 3–4 weeks	1

2—Preparation of Marketing Materials and Buyer List	• Confidentiality agreement for buyers • Confidential information memorandum (CIM) • Teaser and non-disclosure agreement (NDA) • Market research • Develop buyer list • Timeline to completion: 30–60 days	1-2
3—Market Outreach	• Advertise business and screen all potential buyers • Direct outreach • Buyer follow-up and qualification • Bid process • Timeline to completion: 3–6 weeks (ongoing)	2-4
4—Indications of Interest	• Request and receive Indications of Interest (IOI) or Letters of Interest (LOI) from interested buyers • Review with client • Accept and sign offer (likely requiring a period of exclusivity) • Timeline to completion: 4 weeks (ongoing)	4-6

5—Negotiations & Due Diligence	• Help Seller negotiate the sale of the business • Act as a buffer between buyer and seller during negotiations • Offer solutions to overcome impasses • Coordinate and facilitate all buyer / seller meetings and communications • Assemble online data room • Oversee the due diligence process • Timeline to completion: 4–6 weeks	6-7
6—Purchase Agreement	• Act as the lead "mediator" in determining all financial and non-financial terms in the definitive agreement documents • Work with the Company's independent legal counsel to draft all necessary closing documents and related legal documents to affect a sale • Finalize agreement and schedule closing • Timeline to completion: 4 weeks	8-9
7- Closing	• Coordinate and conduct the final closing • Sign all applicable contracts • Exchange of funds—flow of fund sheet	10-12

Pre-M&A Diligence—Seller gathers all relevant business information for the sale process and uploads to an online data room to share with advisor. Getting ready pre-M&A minimizes time pressure in the diligence phase with the buyer.

Indication of Interest—An IOI outlines the proposed terms of the offer at a very high level. It will generally cover price, transition period, and a timeline for due diligence and closing.

Letter of Intent—An LOI includes more details than an IOI. The terms of the LOI will be used in an asset purchase agreement. An LOI allows you to make a more informed decision on your buyer. An LOI often has language locking out other buyers during the negotiations and due diligence.

Although IOIs and LOIs are traditionally non-binding, they can have binding language that you need to understand. Before signing, it is important to review these documents with your attorney for legal guidance.

If you have received an offer from a potential buyer, how do you know if that offer is the one to accept? It's like marriage. You need to be sure.

5. Advisors aim to maximize your deal terms.

It is important to complete a valuation with an intermediary to determine a "real world" business value and target price range. If your asking price is set too high, it may be challenging to attract buyers. If you set the price too low, you may end up leaving money on the table.

Lenders will require their own third-party valuation to ensure that the cash flows of the business can service the debt.

If you've sold a home before, you might think that selling your business is similar. It's very different. The buyer and seller agreeing on a sale price and closing date is just scratching the deal surface. Intermediaries will work on your behalf to maximize your transaction terms.

In addition to purchase price, there are dozens of items to be negotiated including:

- Is an asset sale or stock sale more beneficial?
- Do you need to provide seller financing?
- How long should you allow for due diligence?
- Do you need to stay after the sale to train? Will you be paid?
- Do you get to keep the cash you have in the bank?
- What about your accounts receivable?
- Do you get to keep your personal vehicle?
- Should you let the buyer speak to your employees?
- Should you allow a portion of closing proceeds to be placed in escrow?
- How will the purchase price be allocated for tax purposes?
- Is an earnout beneficial? How should it be structured?

Consider if you were going to sell your home by yourself as for sale by owner. In the housing market, it can be done. Buyers can look at the house, see the size of the property, view the tax assessment, see the condition of the roof, kitchen, bathrooms, and so on. These are all observable, tangible things.

In a business, most of the things to assess are intangibles like the financials. If you're trying to sell it by yourself, how do you represent its value? Unlike real estate transactions, private company transactions are not regulated. The terms of a private company transaction are defined by the parties doing the deal. There are no guidelines or regulations on what must be included. If you don't have the proper advice, you can close a deal not realizing potential value was left on the table.

Buyers are very careful especially if they are going to operate your business as a standalone-entity. Acquisition entrepreneurs may not have other company synergies to offset overhead or accelerate revenue. They must be able to service the business debt and ensure that the cash flow supports the required return on investment.

"Pitfalls to Avoid When Selling Your Business"
Paul Visokey, President, Stony Hill Advisors
Succession Stories Podcast E84[56]

Paul Visokey is the Founder and President of Stony Hill Advisors, an M&A Advisory firm specializing in transactions in the lower middle market. Selling your business is one of the most important transactions of your life. It's an intensive undertaking that requires the right team of collaborators to guarantee success.

Laurie Barkman:
We've done the valuation on our company and now we're thinking about putting it on the market. Are we going to go about this on our own as a business owner? What are some of the pitfalls of some business owners who have gone about the "For Sale By Owner" path?

Paul Visokey:
Excellent question because most of our clients, the baby boomers, have been in their business thirty years. They've never done this before; they have no expertise. You may sell three or four houses in your lifetime. You're selling your business once, and it's the most valuable asset you have, especially if it's the end of your career and you're selling to retire. You want to get the best advice and get the best offer you can. To do it on your own is amazing, that just doesn't make sense to me.

We get asked sometimes by a potential seller if they have someone interested in buying their company. We offer facilitation services to help them execute the transaction with our advice and oversight of what's happening—including the valuation so they know what their business is worth—and what they should be asking. It really makes a difference. It's important that you don't to do this on your own or with just your accountant or your attorney. They can do part of the job, but there's much more to it. We work collaboratively with accountants and attorneys because we all have something to add to the process.

Laurie Barkman:
There's a lot of time that goes into selling. There's the back and forth on commu-nications and there's also confidentiality. It's hard to know when to share with your team. That can be a distraction, but you have to interest them at the right time. That can be a pitfall too, especially if you're running a process on your own.

Paul Visokey:
It's absolutely true. We're often asked, "What should I tell anybody that reports to me?" The answer is it depends really on how trustworthy they are to keep it quiet, and how necessary they are to stay on board. I have a client, who is giving phantom stock, a piece of the action if the business is sold, so the key employee gets a part of the transaction value. Because he needs to keep him on board, to stay on. He put a time on the vesting of the phantom stock, like two or three years, so the buyer knows this key individual is going to stay involved in the business. Those are factors that come into play. That's where the facilitation comes in. We analyze the circumstances around the transaction and help the seller make the best decisions along the way.

Laurie Barkman:
We need to figure out who these potential buyers might be. Why don't we talk a little bit about some of the pitfalls in this phase?

Paul Visokey:
I mentioned earlier that we often find strategic acquirers. There is a potential for an economic buyer so there is a listing process. You can put the business on the market in a confidential way and let people find it. But that's kind of posting and hoping that they find it.

We identify interested buyers and it can be a competitor. In some cases, clients don't want their competitor, so we'll make a list and sometimes it gets scratched. It can be a vertical market integration, if someone in your industry is making acquisitions that's helping them grow so they're buying down and adding on to their company, which is often the case with private equity; there's platforms and there's add-ons. They can meet a supplier who wants to ensure that they have customers for their products and services, and so on. We analyze the potential marketplace and use our tools and databases to identify the targets. We send them teasers which like the listing, is non-descript. It doesn't reveal the name the company. We have to protect the confidentiality, but it's enough to be interested. It goes back to the NDA and starting a process with that potential buyer. There's a number of avenues we take, depending on the type of business and the opportunity to find the right buyer but you have to understand the marketplace to be able to do that.

Laurie Barkman:

It can take a decent amount of back and forth is why having an intermediary is helpful. I find in my experience working with sellers, it takes them away from their day-to-day, from their team, their focus. It's a lot that we put on ourselves and that's a key part of the process. One of my clients was trying to determine why should he hire an M&A advisor. He spoke with a business owner who told him, "They're providing a level of service on things that you just wouldn't want to be doing. It's very different from running your business day-to-day." Now that I've been working with him, he told me that story because I think he appreciates what I'm doing for him and there's a lot happening behind the scenes that he knows I'm doing on his behalf.

What are some of the deal terms that might be included to make sure that the transition is successful?

Paul Visokey:

Most of these occur in the negotiation, where there might be a mismatch on price where a buyer makes an offer, and the seller wants more, so you can close that gap with things like earnouts, and seller notes. Other aspects come up, non-compete agreements, a compensation agreement that you're going to stay on for X number of years, sometimes even a minority interest in in the acquirer's business. We provide guidance on what is common and recommended in certain circumstances, because it's important to understand, to feel the difference in the attention of the negotiation to what if it's an easy negotiation, then you can resolve these things quickly. If it's a tense negotiation, then you've got to hold your ground and make sure you don't get rolled over.

After the acquisition is completed, there are issues of integration. Today the human capital component of a transaction is becoming so important and has to be thought of in advance of the closing. In a strategic sense, the buyer and seller have a population of employees and there might be an overlap. Or it might be different HR policies. It might be different compensation plans they merge. That's a tricky process too. There's a lot of work and this is not an easy job from beginning to end.

Types of Transactions: Asset or Stock Sale

An asset sale is the purchase of individual assets and liabilities. A stock sale is the purchase of the owner's shares of a corporation. Each type of sale is structured differently. Generally, the tax implications and potential liabilities are the primary concerns for both business buyers and sellers.

In an asset sale, the business transfers its assets to the buyer's entity once the asset purchase agreement (APA) is executed. The seller retains legal ownership of the original corporate entity.

In an asset sale, the business is sold on a "debt-free, cash-free basis," meaning the seller would assume any cash or debts as well as non-direct assets (e.g. real estate). The buyer chooses which assets and liabilities to purchase. Because buyers are often only interested in real assets, items like accounts payable and mortgage payments are often not part of an APA. Asset sales typically include the net working capital (accounts receivable less accounts payable).

In an asset sale, the assets can be tangible, such as real estate, inventory, fixtures, and equipment. You can also transfer intangible assets including:

- Customer lists
- Telephone numbers
- Trade names
- Trade secrets
- Warranties
- Goodwill
- Licenses
- Leases

As discussed in Chapter 9, it is good to have a list of what assets your company can transfer and whether these are attractive to potential buyers.

Now let's jump back to a stock sale. A stock sale allows the buyer to directly purchase shares in your company. This is how many well-established businesses are passed on to a new owner.

A stock sale means you can transfer the entire entity including all the assets and liabilities. Of course, this depends on the terms in the purchase agreements. For example, the buyer may ask you to settle some of the company's liabilities or debts before closing the deal. Generally the transfer process is simpler in a stock sale.

When it comes to other liabilities, these may be big risks in a buyer's eyes:

- Defined benefit pension plans—these obligations scare nearly any buyer
- Environmental liabilities—anything where the rules are changing, and it could become very expensive, not easily fixed, or cannot be accurately predicted
- Threatened litigation
- Patent infringement—do you have a patent that you can't hold on to or is difficult to defend
- Warranty risk—rework pending or product liability risk you don't know about yet (incurred but not reported). Even if the buyer indemnifies, this risk could impair their business going forward and might have to pay for it directly or indirectly.

A stock sale can only be performed on fully incorporated entities like a C Corporation, or sometimes an S Corporation. Stock sales are not meant for sole proprietorships, LLCs, and partnerships. If you're trying to sell a C Corporation, a stock deal has more favorable tax treatment at the lower capital gains rate.

It's worth noting that if you own an LLC, you could choose to sell a partial stake of your ownership interest. You will want to consult a tax professional to ensure that you are paying the appropriate amount of taxes on the money you receive versus your original investment.

In an asset sale, ordinary income tax rates apply to the sale of physical assets. The lower capital gains tax rate will apply to intangible assets like goodwill.

Although stock sales are attractive for sellers, they may be less so for buyers. Many prospective buyers prefer asset deals. By purchasing assets, buyers get to avoid liabilities and benefit from a step-up in the asset tax basis generating tax deductions on amortization or depreciation. An asset sale is the most common deal structure for companies in the lower middle market.

If you're considering a sale to a third-party, it is recommended that you seek the assistance of a business broker experienced in finding buyers, managing paperwork, and navigating the process. You're likely to close the deal more quickly than if you are selling a business by yourself.

"Skills to Build Your Business Are Not Same to Sell It"
Jeffrey Feldberg, CEO and Co-Founder, Deep Wealth Experience
Succession Stories Podcast E105[57]

Laurie Barkman:
The process of making your company ready to sell makes it a better company. What were some examples of things you needed to work on?

Jeffrey Feldberg:

As business owners, we cannot master something that we've never done before. For most business owners selling a business, that's really something foreign to us. The skills that built our business are not the same skills to sell it. Some people may not know that. One of the biggest take-aways was to surround myself with the best world class, absolute best advisors. Laurie, I didn't know you at the time, I probably should have. You would have made that much more of a difference for me back in the day. If you're thinking about selling your company, get Laurie on board and have her help you prepare. Then do the whole process and the competitive bid. You have one chance, don't gamble with your future. You want to stack the odds in your favor. You don't want to level the playing field, you want to tilt the playing field.

The other big thing, where a lot of business owners find themselves, the business doesn't run without them. I don't care if you're a 20-person company and you don't have a management team, or you're a 200-person company and you do have a management team. Often, nothing happens without the owner and that's a big, big impediment. Buyers want to do two things. First and foremost, minimize risk. Second, they want to maximize return on investment. They're mutually exclusive. When the business doesn't run without the business owner, there's no management team that's independent, that's a big red flag. One of two things will happen. There won't be a deal. Or the value, the enterprise value, gets penalized, and goes down, down, down.

Consider that 80 percent companies that go on the market will not sell. Of the two out of ten businesses that sell, many will receive a lower multiple or sale price due to factors that include poor or nontransferable intangible assets. Similar to a buyer's market in real estate, the private capital market will swing in favor of those acquiring versus those selling. Only the most attractive and ready businesses will move into the next stage of their life cycle. Can you afford to be one of the 80 percent that will not sell?

There are several reasons why deals don't make it to the closing table:

1. Seller's price expectations are unrealistic
2. Bad financial recordkeeping
3. Negative changes in business performance
4. Seller change of heart
5. Buyer decides to leave during diligence because of unforeseen or undisclosed facts
6. Buyer unable to secure financing

Having a business that is sell-ready can help you avoid these potential pitfalls.

Ready to Sell Versus Sell-Ready

I am often asked how long it takes to get a business ready for exit. As you may expect, the answer is "it depends." Think about your starting point. It's like making a New Year's resolution to be healthier and more fit. How much time will it take? What will you need to do?

It can take three to five years to improve the business financials, improve transferability, and determine which exit options are the best fit for you. Readying for a sale process can take a while.

To be sell-ready means you've gone through the preparedness process we're covering in this book. You've done the work to understand your value drivers, understand how you compare versus your peers, and punch above your weight class on valuation. Or will a buyer offer you a discounted price due to perceived risks?

The best way to start is to baseline where your company is today across the value drivers and risk factors described in these pages. Discover your business readiness score by visiting: www.mytransitionscore.com.

Getting a business valuation is also an excellent way to baseline what your company is worth today. Many M&A intermediaries and accounting firms offer business valuations as a stand-alone service. A benefit of working with an M&A intermediary on this type of analysis is their understanding of market dynamics which can give you a jumpstart on the selling process if that is your intention.

It is also useful to understand the motivations of strategic buyers or financial buyers. In addition to valuations, I offer clients a market study to understand which value drivers are most important to them and why.

David Wible is a serial entrepreneur. His first business took him over ten years to exit. One of my favorite quotes on *Succession Stories* is from David. "Even if you think you're ready to sell now, you're probably not sell-ready."

David founded Industry Weapon, a digital communications business. He spent six years talking to strategic buyers and private equity groups to build relationships. He built relationships with potential buyers to learn what motivated their investment decisions. He began to understand who might want to acquire his business one day—and why. Even more importantly, he learned why *not*.

He asked questions about the deals that they've done. What do they look for? Size of deals or different criteria? What are elements of the business that are important to them? To that end, he learned that project revenue was less interesting. Potential acquirers would be more interested in his business if it had a recurring revenue model.

Getting this critical feedback enabled him to pivot his business to increase what he calls "VCR" Value Creation Revenue, by increasing recurring revenue and decreasing one-time project-based assignments. He pivoted his business from largely one-time projects to add recurring services with more enterprise value. David successfully sold the company to a strategic buyer based on the growth potential of the recurring revenue model. Ultimately David discovered that it was equally important to have a business that was "ready to sell," as well as being "sell-ready."

Over time, they changed the business model and eventually achieved 40 percent recurring revenue. The moral of the story is that it can be difficult to hear the hard truth. Discovering the hard truth is part one. Part two is deciding what are you going to do about it and taking action.

"Value Creation Revenue and Subscription Businesses"
David Wible, Founder, Industry Weapon
and Work Software
Succession Stories Podcast E68[58]

"I should first tell you that the relationship with the potential buyers happened very early on so it was about a half a decade before we decided to sell that I started having conversations with strategics, growth equity, private equity, with anybody and everybody who would talk to me—investment bankers— just to get a good sense of what the industry looked alike. I've got to tell you, that was so eye opening for me in regard to how my business was going to be valued, and what was a realistic expectation on the sell price.

I think we were worried about even broaching that subject but if we don't get clarity on it as the seller, you hinder yourself in your ability to find the appropriate buyer. Having all those conversations opened my eyes. We were software-as-a-service probably before it was called software-as-a-service. I learned from those bankers that I originally talked to that there were going to be two ways for me to sell the business, a multiple of EBITDA, which would be awful, or a multiple of revenue, which would be amazing. Then it became clear—and I coined the phrase value creation revenue or VCR—from those conversations and realizing that some of the revenue streams that I had that were creating great cash flow and profit to the business weren't going to be calculated in in the sale of the business. That really helped me get my house in order in regard to what revenue I wanted my team to focus on, and what I wanted to focus on. Most importantly, who the buyers were, that I wanted to go after."

If you're looking to get acquired, you need to have the right fit for the buyer.

Recognize that the conversation they're having when you're not in the room:

- What pain points are you solving for them?

- Would they want to buy you, partner with you, or re-build your solution?
- What would it cost them to replicate what you do, and how long would it take?

Having recognition of what makes you different, special, unique. What is additive to them?

A small business can have a high caliber of talent who delivers unique value. You can have a team of three people and be interesting to an acquirer because they want the skill sets that you've developed. That's an "acqui-hire" situation.

If you are considering an exit to a third-party in the future, can you look forward (and backward)? What's the narrative and you might find that if you work backward, you might change your product service mix to better fit potential acquirers in the future.

As Jeffrey Feldberg, CEO of Deep Wealth Experience, says, "Preparation is the gift that keeps on giving."

You don't necessarily know who your future buyer is going to be. You may decide to work with someone like me to help you find a future buyer.

It's like reverse engineering. If you understand the interests of potential buyers, and how to solve their pain points, they will be more motivated to look at your business and offer a compelling price for your solution. With time on your side, you can work these learnings into your Strategic Transition Plan.

The skills that enabled you to build your business are not the same ones to sell it. When you think about it from that perspective, how can you master something on your own that you've never done before? On your own, it's challenging especially if you have only one chance to get it right. This is where you want to have someone like an M&A intermediary to work with you and make a difference.

There can be too much downside if you don't have someone skilled on your side of the table negotiating the deal. Entrepreneurs don't build their businesses on their own. So why would you think about exiting or selling your business on your own?

Even if you're not ready to sell—you're two or three years away from selling—you should consider to speaking with an M&A advisor. I would be happy to talk with you as a starting point.

It takes considerable time and effort to get ready to sell. Waiting until the last minute can be detrimental to you. The more prepared you are, the easier the process will be and the more value you'll receive at closing.

TAKE-AWAYS:

- There's a difference between "ready to sell" and a "sell ready" business.
- Find the right fit with potential buyers by determining what problems you solve for them.
- Work with an M&A advisor to get ready to sell. Waiting until the last minute can be detrimental.
- Get your business readiness score at www.mytransitionscore.com.

MY ACTION PLAN

What will you do to learn more about the process to sell your business?

Action Item	Resources Needed	Start By Date	Complete By Date

CHAPTER 14

PUTTING A STRATEGIC TRANSITION PLAN TOGETHER

It is not the critic who counts; not the man who points
out how the strong man stumbles, or where the doer
of deeds could have done them better. The credit
belongs to the man who is actually in the arena.

THEODORE ROOSEVELT

On each episode of *Succession Stories*, I ask guests to share a favorite quote about entrepreneurship or leadership. Interestingly, the quote most frequently referenced is the "Man in the Arena" by Theodore Roosevelt.

Some say the poignancy of the quote is that as an entrepreneur you make sacrifices. You know what you are trying to do, what your aspiration is, what your vision is, and don't need people telling you what to do. Another said that you take a lot of shots when you're in the lead, and it's a reminder that it's worth staying in the ring and continuing. Another person said it's a reminder not to be afraid of failure. Dust yourself off when you make mistakes and go forward. Go for the dream you have. Go for the bigger why that's important to you in your business, what it is that you really want to become. I chose this quote to bring all these meanings forward and to encourage you.

Throughout this book, you may have uncovered a BHAG ("Big Hairy Audacious Goal") that will generate millions of dollars in enterprise value. On the flip side, you may have gained a better understanding of "ground-floor" action plans to execute.

I believe that a big "why" is getting peace of mind that you've set up your company, and yourself, for a successful transition. Regardless of whether you intend to run your company for the next ten years, or the next two, having a more attractive and transferable business, is not only going to make your company more valuable in the future, but it will be more enjoyable to operate today.

This chapter is a go-to summary for business transition planning. Hopefully you've been using the action planning tools throughout the book and here is how to put it all together.

Action Plan Summary:

1. Establish your transition goals for personal, business, and financial readiness.
2. Understand the value of your business today to determine your "number" and if there's a value gap.
3. Focus on the most impactful value drivers and risk tripwires in your business.
4. Consider multiple exit channels to create more value for your stakeholders.
5. Develop your exit timeline.
6. Get organized! Prepare your financials and pre-diligence materials.
7. Assemble your advisory team.
8. Develop your Strategic Transition Plan.

1 – Establish your transition goals for personal, business, and financial readiness.

Like many entrepreneurs, you may have a high bias for DOING. Hopefully by reading this book, you have made time for THINKING. Develop your vision and goals for transition. When I work with clients on these questions, it can take multiple advisory sessions to refine. Take the time to articulate what's important to you.

- What are your transition planning goals from a personal standpoint?
- What are your financial goals?
- What are your business goals?

Visit mytransitionscore.com to complete assessments for business and personal readiness. Once you complete the confidential surveys, you will receive an overview of your scores and high-level recommendations.

2 – Understand the value of your business today.

The price that a buyer is willing to pay for your business depends on various financial and intangible factors. Your multiple will be based on perceived value and risk. It is important to determine your financial freedom point—a number that funds your retirement if you sold your business. Is there a gap between your "Number" and the valuation estimate? The more time you have to close the gap the better. If your value potential is directionally risking, or declining, this may influence your thinking around exit timing.

3 – Determine most important value drivers and risk factors to address.

There are many factors that drive the value of your business. The key is determining which ones will have the greatest impact. Assessing which drivers matter most to your potential buyers is key to moving the needle.

If you have a written strategic plan, evaluate whether changes are needed to incorporate the concepts presented in this book. What are the things that your company should be working on strategically increase enterprise value? Are they already incorporated into your plan? Consider strengths to capitalize on for growth and differentiation, and address risks that could prevent you from achieving your transition goals.

Hiring a strategic planning facilitator can be a worthwhile investment enabling to you to participate rather than lead the meetings yourself.

4 – Consider multiple transfer channels to create more value for your stakeholders.

In earlier chapters, we covered several important topics related to creating more options for your business succession:

- Thinking about your ideal buyer and who might want to own your business one day.
- Considering the three different categories—strategic, financial, and related buyers. This could open any number of possibilities including competitors, private equity groups, an ESOP, family office investors, your own family members, and your management team.
- Understanding what motivates these buyers and which aspects of your business are valued more highly by them. On the flip side, understanding what would cause potential buyers to run for the hills is also valuable information to know.
- Developing a plan to make your business more transferable and attractive to those transfer channels.
- Evaluating "what should be built" versus "who wants to buy what is already built."

5 – Develop your exit timeline.

It can take time and resources to build value in your business. Use this template to develop a timeline to gain clarity on milestones, goals, key strategies, and what life stage (or age) as potential reasons behind your decisions.

A watch-out of developing a transition timeline based primarily on your age is that you might wait too long. What if your business really isn't transferable or not quite ready for a new owner? Recall that a business that is not transferable will have less value, which could hurt your retirement.

Over the years of working with small to midsize clients, I've seen this happen and it's heartbreaking. They worked their whole life. They didn't go to all the sports matches with their kids, they didn't take vacations, and they meshed their identity with their business. When they've decided to sell, they're disappointed to learn that their company may not be worth what they think due to low transferability or other risk factors.

I have a client with a ten-year exit time horizon. There are different milestones he wants to achieve to enable him to achieve the life and legacy he envisions with the team, clients, and communities he serves. We developed a transition timeline that incorporates his different life stages and potential exit options along the way.

Here's an example of a high-level exit timeline:

Year	Transition Planning Milestone	Goals: • Revenue • EBITDA • Enterprise Value • Multiple	Key Strategies	Age/Life Stage
0	Strategic Growth Plan	• $10M • $1M • $3M • 3X multiple	• Business Development • Geographic expansion	50. Hands-on CEO.
+2	Strategic Transition Plan	• $15M • $2M • $6M • 3X multiple	• Profitability • Succession Planning	52. Kids in high school.

+6	Exit Discussion— internal sale or 3rd party	• $25M • $5M • $20M • 4X multiple	• New President	56. Step back. Kids in college.
+10	Exit Discussion— internal sale or 3rd party	• $30M • $6M • $30M • 5X multiple	• Ownership transition	60. Retire as CEO. Sell majority stake. Serve on Board of company. Focus on philanthropy.

6 – Get organized! Prepare your financials and pre-diligence materials.

The first thing buyers do is evaluate your financials. If you don't have consistently reported and error-free financials, you'll want to put this at the top of your action plan.

Financial Record Keeping

A minimum requirement for your business is to use an electronic book-keeping system such as QuickBooks, or other industry standard accounting system.

If you have a bookkeeper, the most important function they can perform is to make individual entries with details and proper documentation to prove its existence.

Performing these clerical tasks in a consistent basis will save you money and increase your company's value in the long run.

Reviewed or Audited Financials

For many companies in the lower middle market, having reviewed or audited financial statements is often viewed as an expensive obligation to meet bank loan requirements or something that "bigger" companies do.

In the context of value building, and increasing the attractiveness of your business, working with a CPA firm may provide a sizable ROI (return on investment) to increase your company's valuation over time.

A financial review is performed by a certified public accountant (CPA) to provide an evaluation of a business's financial statements, limiting the analysis to analytical procedures and assessment of management. The outcome of a review can only determine the plausibility of financial statements. The analysis determines if they are free from any material misstatements and if they meet generally accepted accounting principles (GAAP). In this way, a financial review provides limited assurance.

The cost of a financial review or audit depends on the condition of your books and records. If your books are immaculate, then the auditors will have an easier time reviewing them and conducting their tests to determine that everything is correct and presented fairly. Many CPAs may be able to conduct the review when your taxes are prepared and roll the costs together.

An audited financial statement is a financial statement that has been prepared in accordance with GAAP and has been audited by an independent CPA in accordance with generally accepted auditing standards and includes footnotes to the financial statements.

The audit team will review the company's documents, processes, and procedures. Then they will issue an opinion on whether the financial statements are presented fairly, in all material aspects, in accordance with the financial reporting framework. In contrast to the limited assurance provided by a financial review, a financial audit provides a reasonable amount of assurance.

For this reason, when a CPA performs an audit, they accept the liability associated with their work. If a company that was audited is found to be fraudulent, then the CPA firm or individual professional may lose their license and credibility. The CPA firm is open to civil lawsuits and face legal fees and penalties. The cost of a financial audit typically exceeds $10,000 because of the time to required perform an audit. An audit is unique to each company and is customized to every set of books provided by a company to understand and determine the risk involved.

If your business is not required to have an audit, but you would like a thorough analysis of your financial records, you may choose to have a financial review.

Benefits of having reviewed or audited financial statements:

1. Value: Companies that have annual financial statement reviews or audits are generally more profitable and better managed than companies that do not undergo a review or audit. Having reviewed or audited financial statements provides a level of assurance to a buyer or investors about the company's net profit, sales, and revenue growth, debt level, profit margin, and free cash flow. This makes a company more valuable and attractive to third parties.
2. Attractiveness: It becomes easier to attract investors, buyers, and lenders, if a company can demonstrate to outside parties that their financial statements are reliable. During the due diligence process, buyers want to see a solid history of financial statements, usually three years, before making a decision to purchase a company.
3. KPIs: Learn what profitable companies do well, and what unprofitable companies do poorly. Gain insight about best practices in your industry and KPIs. Benchmark your company's performance versus your peers to determine if you're punching above or below your weight class.
4. Growth: Evaluate operating margins to understand the impact of your company's pricing strategy and operating efficiencies. Useful to evaluate the costs associated with growing the business and where adjustments can be made. Determine whether your company's cash position is likely to improve or decline.

5. Risk Management: Ensure compliance with regulatory reporting and accounting standards. Address internal control issues.

"How to Prepare for Sell Side Diligence"
Jeffrey Ford, Founding Partner,
Grossman, Yanak and Ford
Succession Stories Podcast E86[59]

Laurie Barkman:

Let's take the scenario of a company that is interested in selling, and maybe they have some suitors. There are letters of intent on the table and one of those is chosen to move forward in a process where we want to get to a purchase agreement. Where does due diligence fall?

Jeffrey Ford:

For buy-side due diligence, the buyer wants to be ready and typically performs their buy side quality of earnings or financial due diligence during the exclusivity period that typically kicks off with a letter of intent being signed and agreed upon in some way. When one does that on the buy side, it's time pressure, you have forty-five, sixty, ninety days of exclusivity, and it's intense and highly focused.

Conversely, on the sell-side, I think it should be approached very differently than that. I think on the sell-side, you want to be prepared well in advance of a letter of intent. You want to walk through it. You want to get things out in the open when you have more time. I realize that exit planning advisors say to start three years before you want to sell. From a financial diligence side sell side Q of E, six months to one year is fine. If you're doing your sell-side diligence, when you have an LOI from a suitor, you really are scrambling. Your back is against the wall. You have given several advantages to the other team. That doesn't mean you can't win. I think our role and your deal team's role is to help you to amass as many advantages on your side of the table as you possibly can.

Laurie Barkman:
What does Q of E, or Quality of Earnings, entail?

Jeffrey Ford:
Q of E goes a little bit deeper into the financial side to be sure. It talks about the industry, talks about strengths and weaknesses in the industry, talks about the purported strengths and weaknesses of the company at hand in this case, the seller's company. It typically focuses on things that would be of interest to a buyer. Think about what a buyer would be excited about or worried about. That's how the seller should be thinking.

Most sellers underestimate the number of things a buyer would be worried about. A seller lives in there. They know the risk, they don't think about it. They've been comfortable with it for a decade or two. But if they were in the other chairs, they would be worried about a lot of things. They want to know the story. They also know that sellers tend to embellish this story. The sell side Q of E is saying, "How do we lay something out there to facilitate the buyer's process? How do we calm the buyer's fears? How do we tell them a concise, accurate story about the financial situation of this company?" If there are audited or reviewed statements, which are very helpful, we'll refer to them. They will not be incorporated in their entirety, but they will be referred to. We will have a section on working capital. What is the normal working capital that we might need to run this business? Sometimes it's cyclical, sometimes it's consistent.

Sometimes there are significant concentrations of customers, almost everybody thinks customer concentration. If 80 percent of your business has one customer, you better have a good story as to how you keep that customer. Similarly, the concentrations aren't always the customer. If you require something for your secret sauce, and it's available only in one place. Very important to tell that story.

We did a sell side Q of E work four or five years ago for a company. A neat company, great product, great margin. Their margin was enhanced because of this minuscule, inexpensive item that really allowed them to achieve tolerances that excelled beyond their competition, and drove their premium margins, which in turn, of course, drove their premium price. That little widget was only available from one source. That would worry a buyer a great deal. We addressed that in the sell side Q of E, we addressed the continuity arrangement. The legal team also helped with bringing calm to that situation and really averted a challenging conversation later.

You introduced a very important question. Other concentrations might be with who owns the sales relationships. Oftentimes, it's the business owner. Are they transferable? Will those customers talk to the new owners? Will they be loyal? Or would they merely go to their second favorite provider? My favorite is one we didn't see coming, but we stumbled upon it. We were deep in the due diligence process in the sale, and we learned that most of the salespeople had virtually no book of business. A super majority of the sales book of business was with one salesperson. We said, "Can we talk to that salesperson?" "He only comes in a few days a week, because he's over seventy-five years old."

That would worry me if I were a buyer. Put yourself in the buyer's shoes. Now the seller in this case would think about it because they were used to dealing with this gentleman. Over the course of several decades, the salesperson was highly competent, highly dedicated, highly successful, and it wasn't even on their minds. Putting ourselves on the side of the buyer, we were part of the collaborative team that came up with the transition plan from the more experienced salesperson to what would happen. How do we transfer these relationships? In this case, he was willing to commit several years to a buyer to also facilitate that transition. I will say completely directly and bluntly, if that was not done ahead of time, if we were serving the buyer side, we would have made that a big, big deal. We would have made sure that significantly informed the negotiations of purchase price and other terms of that agreement. A Q of E really helps to get several concerns on the table and also opportunities.

Pre-Diligence

Hopefully by now, you've accepted the fact that one day you will leave your company. If you leave your business sooner than expected, through an unexpected circumstance, will your heirs or partner be left with a mystery?

You know how hard it can be to find something that you last looked at eons ago, somewhere in your computer system. "Where did I save that file?" Now imagine that your grieving partner or loved ones need to locate these documents.

On a more uplifting note of encouragement, imagine that you're in the process of selling your business to a new owner. You could spend hours searching for information.

"Selling Your Company"
John Warrillow, Author of The *Built to Sell* Trilogy, and Founder of The Value Builder System
Succession Stories Podcast E82[60]

"The notion of pre-diligence, doing the heavy lifting to make sure you've got all your documents together is going to be important. I interviewed a couple named Michael Houlihan and Bonnie Harvey, the founders of Barefoot Winery. An American winery, they got their wine in all the Trader Joe's in the United States. It's a huge success story, one of the largest, if not the largest independent wine makers in the United States when they decided to sell.

They looked around at the landscape of people who would likely buy their company. The most likely strategic acquirer was E & J Gallo, which at the time was the largest wine maker in the United States, part of a large conglomerate. They said E & J Gallo is the natural acquirer. One thing that most people would do at that point is reach out to someone at E & J Gallo and say, "Hey, we're maybe making a decision the next twelve months, would you be interested?" That's one way to approach it, but they chose a different route. They chose to do all their pre-diligence upfront. Pre-diligence means getting all your supplier contracts into a binder or virtual data room, getting all your sales information, all your legal documents, your rent, all the things that you need to demonstrate due diligence to an acquirer in advance.

I said to Bonnie and Michael, "Why did you do that? Why didn't you just wait till due diligence until at least you had an offer on the table?" He said, "Well, two reasons. Number one, we wanted the diligence process to be as smooth as possible to make sure that anything that came up would have been handled preemptively." Fair enough. The second reason, I think was brilliant. He said, "The second reason, we put all the binders together and came to E & J Gallo very buttoned-up, very polished. In a subtle way it communicated to E & J Gallo that we were ready for the dance. We were ready for the prom. If they didn't want to take us to the prom, that was their prerogative, but we were going to the prom." Meaning, we were going to sell this company and if E & J Gallo chose to drag their feet or not make an offer, the veiled threat without them having to play hardball, was they were going to go to somebody else. I think that is such an important strategy for owners.

t's not like selling a car or selling a house where you can put it on the market and see what offers to get in and take it back off. Selling a business is not like that. You do irreparable harm if you try to sell it to test the waters, so to speak. I think what you want to do is be very thoughtful about your pre-diligence. When you make the decision to go to market, you want to do your due diligence. Again, it's going to make everything run much more smoothly and it is also going to communicate to the acquirers that you're serious. That you're going to find a buyer that may be them, but it may not be if they're not interested. I think it's an important thing to do. It goes back to what you need to do in the twelve months leading up to a sale. Hire somebody like yourself, or an accountant, or consultants. Do pre-diligence because it's a hugely overlooked strategy and it can play very well to the value of your company."

Time kills deals so you don't want to waste time hunting down key documents that could delay diligence, or worse, a closing date. If you get organized, and stay organized, you will be rewarded with less stress and a better outcome.

One of my podcast guests successfully sold his business without the help of an M&A advisor. Off-air he told me that he wished he had a due diligence list to work from proactively himself. He would have liked to get ready when he wasn't under a time clock. He found the process burdensome when he had to comply on a deadline.

Hearing this insight, I've decided to include a diligence list in this handbook. Due diligence request lists can vary based on the deal factors, industry, buyer preferences, etc. so use this one as a starting point. Use it to organize key information that may be needed in the future for due diligence.

As your transition sherpa, I would be remiss if I didn't suggest some pro-tips for getting and staying organized:

1. Create an organized folder structure for your important company records.
2. Use a logical hierarchy that gives every important file a home, making things easy to find.
3. Store documents on a server or shared online location, not on your personal computer.
4. Consider using sub-folders if there are different versions of your documents: Final, Draft, and Archive.
5. Use good file naming conventions. Use clear, descriptive file names that make it easy to identify what's in the file. Here are a few best practices:
   ◦ For dates, use YYYYMMDD [e.g. 20230314] or YYM-MDD [e.g. 230314] format, so dates stay in chronological order
   ◦ Use sequential numbering (01, 02, instead of 1, 2)
   ◦ Avoid special characters (like ~! @ # $ %)
   ◦ Use underscores (file_name) or dashes (file-name) instead of spaces (file name)

Getting your pre-M&A data room organized is one of the first things we do in sell side engagements. We create an internal data room with all the items listed. It is one of the key pieces to being sell-ready.

7 – Assemble your business owner advisory team (BOAT).

Entrepreneurs don't build a company on their own. So why not plan your business transition and exit strategy with trusted experts in your corner. Credit to Jonathan Goldhill, business coach and author of the *Disruptive Successor*, for introducing me to the "BOAT" analogy—a business owner advisory team—to help you be successful. Advisors on your BOAT will help you row the oars in the right direction at the right speed. Choose people with expertise to help you make decisions about how to transition your company on your terms.

Consider the different types of advisors you might engage:

- M&A intermediaries—exit value coaching, valuations, seller representation, buy-side engagements for acquisitions
- Business Coaches—strategic planning, growth, innovation, management succession, sales, post-acquisition integration
- Board Members—CEO succession planning, transition planning, governance
- Insurance Brokers—contingency planning, risk management
- Financial and Investment Advisors—financial planning, asset management
- Accountants—reporting, valuations, tax, compliance, financial reviews, audits, deal diligence
- Attorneys—estate planning, governance, M&A deal transactions, deal diligence

As covered in prior chapters, the process of selling a business is complex. The "urgency of now" will always take precedent as you run your business day-to-day. The skills required to sell your company are not the same as the ones needed to build it.

You probably have a favorite football team, mine is the Pittsburgh Steelers. Everyone needs a good quarterback, especially when it comes to managing an exit value process.

As an M&A intermediary I serve in the quarterback role, working with other BOAT advisors in a collaborative way to provide high impact guidance. Knowing the various intricacies, we work together to make the best deal possible. It's important to engage experienced advisors as early as possible to achieve the vision you have in mind.

Recall that a business that is not transferable will have less value. You're working hard to grow your business, provide for your family, and create a legacy. It is not going to feel great, and will not be a good situation, if you're expecting the sale of your business to fund your retirement but it is far from it. Working with your BOAT is one way to ensure you get the guidance you need on your journey.

8 – Develop your Strategic Transition Plan.

There's an old saying, "Are you working in your business or on your business?" If you want your transition to be successful, you must work on it, you just can't let it happen. If you haven't spent the time to prepare the business, you're going to potentially face a lot of issues. Make time today so you will have options tomorrow. It's always better to be prepared.

You work hard. Have a plan to create the value in your business that you so deserve.

- Where are the big risks in the business, and how can you address them?
- What strengths can you capitalize on?
- What is your business differentiation?
- What would make your business more profitable and improve cash flow?

- Who should own your company one day, and what would make your company more attractive to them?
- Could your business transfer to a new owner and continue to thrive?
- What are growth and innovation opportunities?
- Do you have processes documented and a team in place to execute?
- What diligence information will potential acquirers want to know?
- Are your financials in order?
- What is your business worth today, and what value would you like to see in the future?
- How can you transition from your business in a happy and satisfying way?
- How do you measure up on key value drivers versus your industry peers?

Business transition planning involves understanding where the business is today from a strategic standpoint, to where you want to be. You don't have all have to have all the answers. It's about envisioning the potential end state and what the options are along the way.

I've created a process that I call Strategic Transition Planning to maximize the value of your company.

It takes the methodology of strategic planning, and it layers in the steps of the transition and exit value process outlined throughout the chapters of this book. Working together, we'll get our arms around what could catapult you forward, and what might hold you back.

Strategic Transition Planning is a circular business planning process—looking forward and looping backward. It's like time travel to see your business through a different lens from value building to succession.

Using best practices of strategic planning, you will set a vision, values, goals, strategies, and action plans for your business transition. You'll develop a big-picture timeline; identify key metrics; leverage your BOAT.

Writing down your plan is step one. Execution and alignment is everything. In my experience, it starts with holding yourself accountable to the process.

TAKE-AWAYS:

- Find peace of mind by setting up your company, and yourself, for a successful transition.

- Regardless of whether you intend to run your company for the next ten years, or the next two, having a more attractive and transferable business, is not only going to make your company more valuable in the future, but it will be more enjoyable to operate today.

- Put together a Strategic Transition Plan using the frameworks presented in this book:

    1. Establish your transition goals for personal, business, and financial readiness.

    2. Understand the value of your business today to determine your "number" and if there's a value gap.

    3. Focus on the most impactful value drivers and risk tripwires in your business.

    4. Consider multiple exit channels to create more value for your stakeholders.

    5. Develop your exit timeline.

    6. Get organized! Prepare your financials and pre-diligence materials.

    7. Assemble your advisory team.

MY ACTION PLAN

What will you do to put a business transition plan together?

Action Item	Resources Needed	Start By Date	Complete By Date

FINAL THOUGHTS

When should you start exit value planning? Yesterday was the best time, the second-best time is today. And the third best time is tomorrow. There really is no reason why you shouldn't start now. Strategic Transition Planning and all the concepts in this book will enable you to run a more profitable, enjoyable business to reward you for all your hard work.

At the beginning of this book, I shared my mission of guiding entrepreneurs through the complex process of increasing company value and working with you to let it go when you're ready. Because the focus of this book is on your future business transition, one might say that it is leading you to think about the "end."

On the contrary, I think about transition as letting go of your "now" to start your "next."

I want you to be successful throughout your entrepreneurial journey. Are you focused only on what is in front of you today? Just like in chess, if you are a couple moves ahead, your chances of winning will dramatically increase.

Your business may be more like a cruise ship than a speed boat when it comes to change. To make a big turn, it will take longer but can be done. Take the time to reverse engineer and "begin with the end in mind." If you're interested in selling to a third-party, or passing to the next generation, you need to make sure that you have a well-run business someone wants to take over.

The most common benefit that transition and exit value planning brings you is clarity.

What I see in my practice is that business owners feel relief by having a strategic transition framework and a process to move forward. I hope that this book enables you to find clarity as you make decisions.

Thanks for taking me with you on your journey as your business transition sherpa.

Please stay in touch by joining the community of business owners who are working from transition to transaction at:

www.TheBusinessTransitionHandbook.com.

ACKNOWLEDGMENTS

There are many people I would like to thank and acknowledge who have supported me on my journey.

To my family, Martin, Caroline, and Lars, your endless support means everything to me. To my parents, Cynthia and Allen, thank you for giving me the love of learning and for cheering me on throughout my business transitions.

To my team at JWC Publishing, Tim Jacobs, Daron Christopher, Heidi Caperton, and Laura Kaiser, thank you for your expert guidance throughout the development process.

To my colleagues and team members at SmallDotBig, Stony Hill Advisors, and Carnegie Mellon University Tepper School of Business, thank you for sharing a passion for entrepreneurship.

Thank you to my growing list of *Succession Stories Podcast* guests for sharing your experiences and guidance including: Lexi Grant, Regina Beatty, Bruce Werner, Mike Stemple, Anna Felix, Ben Rizzo, Joel Valentine, Christopher Weir, Tim Tannert, Misty See Meschter, Don See, Cliff Spolander, Stephen Bollinger, Shanice Miller, Tsitsi Mutendi, Bill

Prinzivalli, Jonathan Goldhill, A.J. Lawrence, Rebecca Monet, Zachary Green, Jeffrey Feldberg, Kristi Posluszny, Fred Kaplan, Mark Fujiwara, Jennifer Ake Marriott, Troy Trewin, Meredith Meyer Grelli, Gabriela Isturiz, Sarah Dusek, Deena Chochinov, Ronald Skelton, Per Sjöfors, Rocky Lalvani, Jerry Cahn, Scott Snider, Nicole Jansen, Marcia Riner, Jeffrey Ford, Nana Bonsu, Mark Brandt, John Warrillow, Andrew Cabasso, Daniel Van Der Vliet, Mark Kravietz, Craig Clickner, Carrie Bohlig, Lisa Laird-Dunn, Gerard Dunn III, Jon Dwoskin, Nelson Anderson, Kevin Urrutia, Dave Eichenlaub, Corey Kupfer, Paul Visokey, JT Kostman, Dann Scheiferstein, Tana Greene, Lloyd Wolf, Neil Sahota, William Yanakos, Christopher Yanakos, Hal Riley, Karen Norheim, Kristy Britsch, Julie Ann Sullivan, Bonnie Artman Fox, Kent Johnson, Kelly Henry, Danielle Julia Cuomo, Stephanie Scheller, Beth Armknecht Miller, Alex Panosian, Christopher Brodman, Amy Franko, Darren Gleeman, Alisa Spector Angelo, Steve Peplin, David Wible, Miche Jean, Kevin Trout, Tricia Staible, Ben Grossman, Jennifer Fondrevay, John Brown, James Richardson, Nikè Anani, Michael Silverman, Kurt Lesker, Kristin Lesker Eisel, Jenna Lesker Lloyd, Phillip Swan, Ann Bernard, Robb McKinney, Tom Hine, Tiffany Castagno, Josh Baron, David Gamble, Bruce Walton, Laura Coe, Jeffrey Walker, Rick Terrien, Janet Wischnia, Cheryl L. Fields, Lou Diamond, Chris Chaney, Elizabeth Blount McCormick, Evan Segal, Sean Ammirati, Ann Dugan, Bradley J. Franc, Mary Richter, James Douglas Austin, Dawn Fuchs Coleman, James Van Buren, Will Knecht, Bobby Zappala, Andy Ellis, Len Caric, Jason Seltzer, Joseph Bute, Brian Baum, Michael Schoedinger, Jill Hofmans, Chris Cynkar, Shelley Taylor, Jim Rooney, and Tony Uphoff.

Thank you to everyone who sharpened my thinking, and to my friends who read early drafts to help me make this a better book: Sam Gerard, Dave Mawhinney, Paul Visokey, and Henry DeVries.

To my clients, thank you. It's a privilege to be your business transition sherpa.

NOTES

1. Value Builder System™, Freedom Point, 2021

2. BEI Business Owner Exit Survey, 2019

3. U.S. Bureau of Labor Statistics, Business Employment Dynamics, Table 7. Survival of Private Sector Establishments by Opening Year, March 2022

4. BizBuySell Insight Report, 2017

5. BEI 2016 Business Owner Survey Report, https://www.exitplanning.com/blog/what-are-business-owners-thinking-and-doing-about-their-exits

6. The Value Builder System, The Overlooked Owner: A Key Factor in Determining Business Value

7. https://smalldotbig.com/succession-stories-podcast/73-launching-a-family-office-with-alex-panosian-cw-growth-partners/

8. https://smalldotbig.com/succession-stories-podcast/e10-entrepreneurial-resilience-len-caric-ceo-uncle-charleys-sausage/

9. The Value Builder System, 2021

10. https://smalldotbig.com/succession-stories-podcast/97-creating-a-business-that-can-thrive-without-you-meredith-meyer-grelli/

11. https://www.forbes.com/sites/forbescoachescouncil/2020/06/18/delegation-the-8020-rule-reimagined-for-entrepreneurs/?sh=5ab8336f3040

12. https://smalldotbig.com/succession-stories-podcast/66-preparing-your-business-for-sale/

13. Exit Planning Institute. *The State of Owner Readiness Survey 2013 National Survey Final Report.* 2013

14. https://smalldotbig.com/succession-stories-podcast/94-finding-purpose-after-selling-the-business-sarah-dusek/

15. The National Federation of Independent Business. Small Business Time Management Survey. 2014.

16. https://smalldotbig.com/succession-stories-podcast/89-make-your-business-independent-of-you-scott-snider-exit-planning-institute/

17. https://smalldotbig.com/succession-stories-podcast/74-obsession-with-succession-beth-miller/

18. https://smalldotbig.com/succession-stories-podcast/111-dont-wait-to-plan-your-exit-strategy-bill-prinzivalli/

19. https://www.investopedia.com/terms/f/four-percent-rule.asp

20. Freedom Point Calculator, The Value Builder System

21. https://smalldotbig.com/succession-stories-podcast/e22-clearing-blurred-lines-of-business-transition-with-chris-chaney/

22. Instagram Revenue and Usage Statistics (2022), Mansoor Iqbal, September 6, 2022, https://www.businessofapps.com/data/instagram-statistics/

23. https://www.wallstreetprep.com/knowledge/lbo-candidate-characteristics/

24. https://smalldotbig.com/succession-stories-podcast/73-launching-a-family-office-with-alex-panosian-cw-growth-partners/

25. https://www.prnewswire.com/news-releases/wilmington-trust-survey-reveals-vast-majority-of-business-owners-unprepared-to-sell-business-or-transition-even-as-many-approach-retirement-age-300953627.html

26. https://smalldotbig.com/succession-stories-podcast/93-acquisition-entrepreneur-buy-side-deals-ron-skelton/

27. https://www.pwc.com/us/en/services/trust-solutions/private-company-services/library/family-business-survey.html

28. https://smalldotbig.com/succession-stories-podcast/64-nextgen-growth-by-acquisition-ben-grossman/

29. https://www.forbes.com/sites/maryjosephs/2018/06/19/fast-facts-on-esops/?sh=6de655242b1b

30. https://smalldotbig.com/succession-stories-podcast/
    succession-stories-e43-debunking-esop-myths-kristy-britsch/

31. Advocacy.sba.gov

32. Pepperdine Private Capital Markets Project, Private Capital
    Markets Report 2021

33. https://smalldotbig.com/succession-stories-podcast/105-skills-to-
    build-your-business-are-not-same-to-sell-it-jeffrey-feldberg/

34. https://smalldotbig.com/succession-stories-podcast/sell-or-
    transition-your-business-podcast/e54-scaling-and-selling-a-
    services-business-kevin-urrutia-ceo-voy-media/

35. https://firstpagesage.com/seo-blog/
    ebitda-multiples-by-industry/#1649799460182-24fd7ced-0113

    Construction Business Valuations & Multiples, https://www.miner-
    vaequity.com/construction-business-valuation-multiples/

    GCA E-Commerce Valuation Outlook Q3 2021, https://gcaaltium.
    com/wp-content/uploads/2021/08/How-the-e-commerce-land-
    scape-has-evolved-in-the-last-18-months-1.pdf

    Engineering Firm Valuations: August 2021, https://cenkuslaw.com/
    buying-selling-engineering-firm-austin-tx-part-2/

    Environment & Climate Change – Transaction Multiples
    2021, https://www.epsilon-research.com/valuation-multiples/
    environment-and-climate-change?sectorId=40020

    Valuation Multiples for Financial Advisories 2020, https://peak-
    businessvaluation.com/valuation-multiples-for-a-financial-advisory/

    Fintech: 2021 Valuation Multiples, https://finerva.com/report/
    fintech-2023-valuation-multiples/

CB Insights' State of Fintech 2021, https://www.cbinsights.com/research/report/fintech-trends-q4-2020/

Healthcare Services M&A: EBITDA Multiple Trends, https://www.buckheadfmv.com/single-post/healthcare-services-m-a-ebitda-multiple-trends

Market Update: Industrial Automation & IOT – Q2 2021, https://www.7mileadvisors.com/quarterly_earning/market-update-industrial-automation-iot-q2-2021/

Mirus Capital M&A Outlook for Internet of Things, https://merger.com/initiating-coverage-mergers-acquisitions-iot/

Taureau Group 2021 M&A Newsletter: Manufacturing Sector, https://www.taureaugroup.com/resource-center/news-articles/manda-newsletter---march-2021#:~:text=EBITDA%20multiples%20for%20all%20manufacturing,a%20premium%20to%20EBITDA%20multiples.

Goldman Sachs Midstream Market Review, chrome-extension://efaidnbmnnnibpcajpcglclefindmkaj/https://www.gsam.com/content/dam/gsam/pdfs/us/en/fund-literature/quarterly-fund-update/GSAM-US-Energy-and-Infrastructure-Quarterly-Update.pdf?sa=n&rd=n

Valuation in the Oil & Gas Industry, https://oilprice.com/specreport/companyvaluation/8

Valuation Multiples for Software Companies 2021, https://microcap.co/valuation-multiples-for-tech-software-companies-2021-updated/

Recruiting and Staffing Company Valuations – June 2021, https://www.linkedin.com/pulse/recruiting-staffing-company-valuations-june-30-2021-bratcher-asa/

Executive Freight Trends Insight, https://www.raymondjames.com/-/media/rj/dotcom/files/corporations-and-institutions/investment-banking/industry-insight/executive_freight_trends_digest.pdf

36. https://smalldotbig.com/succession-stories-podcast/94-finding-purpose-after-selling-the-business-sarah-dusek/

37. https://smalldotbig.com/succession-stories-podcast/86-how-to-prepare-for-sell-side-diligence-jeffrey-ford-grossman-yanak-ford/

38. PWC, "Inside Dell Computer Corporation: Managing Working Capital, 1998, https://www.strategy-business.com/article/9571-

39. https://www.uschamber.com/co/start/strategy/small-business-certifications-guide

40. https://smalldotbig.com/succession-stories-podcast/sell-or-transition-your-business-podcast/e54-scaling-and-selling-a-services-business-kevin-urrutia-ceo-voy-media/

41. https://smalldotbig.com/succession-stories-podcast/99-succession-of-culture-after-tragedy-strikes-jennifer-ake-marriott/

42. https://www.investopedia.com/terms/p/phantomstock.asp

43. https://www.investors.com/news/technology/fb-stock-pummeled-by-apple-ad-changes/#:~:text=That's%20the%20biggest%20one%2Dday,on%20the%20stock%20market%20today.

44. https://www.foodbusinessnews.net/articles/13937-homing-in-on-at-home-eating

45. https://smalldotbig.com/succession-stories-podcast/81-how-to-productize-your-services-andy-cabasso/

46. https://smalldotbig.com/succession-stories-podcast/
    e18-ann-dugan-enterprising-generations/

47. https://hbr.org/2010/03/roaring-out-of-recession

48. https://smalldotbig.com/succession-stories-podcast/
    next-gen-corporate-innovation/

49. https://smalldotbig.com/succession-stories-podcast/80-changing-
    the-family-business-narrative-daniel-van-der-vliet-cornell-
    university-smith-family-business-initiative/

50. https://smalldotbig.com/succession-stories-podcast/110-next-
    generation-disruptive-successor-jonathan-goldhill/

51. https://smalldotbig.com/succession-stories-podcast/
    e40-sustainable-innovation-kent-johnson-ceo-highlights/

52. https://smalldotbig.com/succession-stories-podcast/102-creating-
    the-family-enterprise-of-the-future-nike-anani/

53. https://smalldotbig.com/succession-stories-podcast/59-exit-
    planning-vs-succession-planning-mike-silverman-dentons-cohen-
    grigsby/

54. https://smalldotbig.com/succession-stories-podcast/
    e29-ceo-succession-and-letting-go-bruce-walton-battalia-winston/

55. https://smalldotbig.com/succession-stories-podcast/82-selling-
    your-company-john-warrillow-author-built-to-sell-and-founder-
    the-value-builder-system/

56. https://smalldotbig.com/succession-stories-podcast/84-pitfalls-to-
    avoid-when-selling-your-business-paul-visokey-stony-hill-advisors/

57. https://smalldotbig.com/succession-stories-podcast/105-skills-to-build-your-business-are-not-same-to-sell-it-jeffrey-feldberg/

58. https://smalldotbig.com/succession-stories-podcast/sell-or-transition-your-business-podcast/68-value-creation-revenue-and-subscription-businesses-david-wible-work-software/

59. https://smalldotbig.com/succession-stories-podcast/86-how-to-prepare-for-sell-side-diligence-jeffrey-ford-grossman-yanak-ford/

60. https://smalldotbig.com/succession-stories-podcast/82-selling-your-company-john-warrillow-author-built-to-sell-and-founder-the-value-builder-system/

ABOUT THE AUTHOR

Laurie R. Barkman, CM&AA, MBA, the business transition sherpa, is the former CEO of a $100 million revenue company that was sold to a Fortune 50. As a business transition and acquisition intermediary, Barkman provides a structured process for business owners to plan successful transitions of their companies and let go on their terms. She provides strategic transition planning, business valuations, sell-side, and buy-side intermediary services.

Laurie is an adjunct professor of entrepreneurship at Carnegie Mellon University, and hosts the award-winning podcast *Succession Stories*, where she speaks with hundreds of entrepreneurs who have shared their journeys through succession.

Laurie earned her MBA from Carnegie Mellon University, and Bachelor of Science degree from Cornell University. She received certifications from The Alliance of Mergers & Acquisitions Advisors, The Exit Planning Institute, and The Value Builder System™.

Printed in the USA
CPSIA information can be obtained
at www.ICGtesting.com
CBHW030937270923
1153CB00002B/2/J